Published by

Topical Resources

Acknowledgement

The author and publisher would like to acknowledge the contribution made by the staff and pupils of the following schools during the preparation of this book. All teacher pages have been tested in the classroom. All photographed work has been produced by 6 and 7 year old children working in a classroom situation.

Avondale C.P. School, Darwen.
Bailey's Court Primary School, Bristol.
Beetham C.E. Primary School, Milnthorpe, Cumbria.
Church of the Ascension Primary School, Kingswinford.
Coppice Primary School, Heanor, Derbyshire.
Danesfield School, Medmenham, Bucks.
Griffin Park C.P. School, Blackburn.
Grove Park School, Chiswick.
Hundsford C.E. Primary School, Atherton, Manchester.
Leeming and Londonderry C.P. School, Northallerton.
Middle Barton Primary School, Chipping Norton, Oxfordshire.
Queen Margaret C.P. School, Tewkesbury.
Snape County Primary School, North Yorkshire.
Thameside Primary School, Reading.

Step by Step Art is available from all good Educational Bookshops and by mail order from:

Topical Resources, P.O. Box 329,
Broughton,
Preston,
Lancashire.
PR3 5LT

Topical Resources publishes a range of Educational Materials for use in Primary Schools and Pre-School Nurseries and Playgroups.

For the latest catalogue Tel 01772 863158
or Fax 01772 866153

Printed in Great Britain for "Topical Resources", Publishers of Educational Materials, P.O. Box 329, Broughton, Preston, Lancashire PR3 5LT (Telephone 01772 863158), by T.Snape & Company Limited, Boltons Court, Preston Lancashire.

Typeset by Paul Sealey Illustration & Design, 3 Wentworth Drive, Thornton, Lancashire.

First Published September 1998.

ISBN 1 872977 33 2

Contents

Drawing

Painting

Printing

Collage

Sculpture

Textiles

Introduction

This book is intended for teachers of children in Key Stage One to help them develop their 'pupils' understanding and enjoyment of art, craft and design' (N.C. Art Orders)

It covers the Programmes of Study for Key Stage One and links both Attainment Targets throughout using the same skill- based approach introduced in the first book-Step by Step Art for Nursery/Reception classes.

As in the previous book, the sessions are planned to introduce children to a wide range of tools and techniques, to encourage language and discussion and to develop skills in a sequential series of activities. The areas targeted are drawing, painting, printing, collage, textiles and sculpture which are the content of the National Curriculum Art Document. The visual elements of art i.e. language of the subject, line, tone, texture, pattern etc, are identified in relation to each session, and links are made with the work of other artists, craftworkers and designers, both Western and non-Western.

Each individual session and its extension activities, could be used in isolation, or form part of a progressive series of six lessons that focus on one media area at a time.

The necessary art materials needed for individual sessions are listed at the top of each page, and the complete range of art materials needed for a section, together with the suppliers from whom they can be purchased are listed at the end of each section.

All the sessions have been tried out in schools, and demonstrate the achievement of children using the ideas in the book. To these children and their teachers, I should like to express my appreciation and thanks.

Dianne Williams

Drawing

Drawing

Session One.

Activity Finding and making new lines and line patterns.

Focus Line, pattern and texture.

Equipment Needed

Paper cut to A4 or A3 size - Newsprint or Free Art 80gsm or grey sugar paper. Felt pens thick and thin (black only), black biros, drawing pencils(4b or 6b), plasticene, coloured crayons, oil pastels, and coloured pencils.

Talk About

- Groups of lines that are similar in story book pictures, artist's drawings, and on natural objects,e.g. around a knot in wood; what these lines remind you of e.g. waves, rough grass etc.
- Descriptions/ names for these lines.
- Rolling plasticene to make lines.
- The names of the different drawing media.
- How to hold the different drawing media.

Doing

- Choose one child to start a line group, the others add to it in turn drawing similar lines. The lines can vary only in length, thickness and direction.
- Name the line group, and talk about what it reminds the children of.
- Ask the children to roll out their plasticene and use it to make a line group of their own that is different and to describe their lines.
- Now ask the children to draw several different line groups on paper e.g. a group of spiky lines, a group of loopy lines etc. using thick and thin black felt pens and black biros. Use a different drawing tool for each group. Describe each group of lines.
- Next ask the children to draw groups of lines in response to specific words e.g. lines that stand up straight, lines that squeeze together through a gap etc. Remind the children it must be a group of lines each time, not one line alone.
- Look at and discuss pictures of line groups that make a pattern e.g. a spider's web, fish scales, rain falling in a puddle etc.
- Ask the children to choose one of their line groups and turn it into a pattern.The pattern can go vertically, horizontally or diagonally across the page or even focus around a central point. Remind them that the same line can be used in different directions and in different lengths to make a pattern.

Developing the Idea

- Draw a line group that has long lines that gradually get shorter.
- Draw a line group using the full range of drawing media.
- Talk about how each tool changes the line.
- Encourage the children to explore several line groups in colour on a page using a new colour for each group.
- Draw a multi-coloured line group.
- Draw a line group where the lines are sometimes close together and sometimes far apart.
- From individual line group drawings extend the approach to large scale class/group collections on the same paper. Add names for the line groups alongside the work.

Links with AT2 (Knowledge & Understanding of Other Artists)

Gustav Klimt.
Vincent Van Gogh.
David Hockney (pool paintings).

Drawing

Session Two.

Activity Exploring shapes by adding, altering and linking.

Focus Line, shape and pattern.

Equipment Needed Black felt pens (thick and thin), black biros. Paper cut to A3 or A4 size, Newsprint or Free Art 80 gsm plus smaller pieces for rough sketches and drawings of lace. An assortment of buttons, wood shavings, feathers etc. to be added and altered. Sequins for pattern work. Glue and gluespreaders.

Talk About

- The buttons, wood shavings etc that are going to be used along with drawing; where they will be stuck down leaving space around them.
- How much glue to use and where to put it.
- What these shapes could have added to them and what they could become, e.g. faces, monsters etc.
- Using drawing to add and alter these shapes and where it needs to go.
- Making a line pattern to link similar shapes e.g. as in lace.

Doing

- Choose a button, or other shape and place it on your paper. Try it in several places before you stick it down carefully.
- Look at your shape and think about what you might turn it into. Look at the top, the sides and underneath your shape. Try your ideas on a rough piece of paper.
- You will need to draw different sorts of lines and shapes.
- When you have drawn, added and altered your stuck-down shape to turn it into something new, try adding a background using more shapes and lines.
- Now try another shape picture, this time starting with two or more stuck-down shapes to change.
- Look carefully at the shapes in a piece of lace and how they are joined by a pattern of lines.
- Choose three identical shapes, e.g. sequins, and stick them in a row on a new piece of paper. You need to leave a space between each one.
- Use a pattern of lines to join your shapes together like lace.

Developing the Idea

- From a free choice of a number of different shapes, each child to make what they have chosen into a face using drawing to link and add detail.
- Make a collaborative stuck and drawn picture of e.g. a row of houses.
- Stick several similar shapes down randomly and link them by adding lines and shapes to make an embroidery type pattern.
- Stick several spaced sequins or buttons in a row on a large sheet of paper. One child starts the linking pattern, others in turn continue it. Each link could be similar or totally different in design.

Links with AT2 (Knowledge & Understanding of Other Artists)

Lace.
Doilies.
Indian embroidery.
Embroidered table cloths and textiles.

Drawing

Session Three.

Activity Using tone, finding out about light and dark, by smudging and blending.

Focus Tone.

Equipment Needed Black and white chalk pastel or charcoal and white chalk, A3 or A4 grey sugar paper, white Free Art or Newsprint 80gsm. Drawing pencils (4B-6B), small cut squares of assorted shades of grey, white and black paper, glue and glue spreaders.

Talk About

- What light means and what dark means.
- Places in the room where it is dark and places where it is light.
- Places in story book pictures and artist's pictures that are dark and those that are light and how you can tell.
- Newspaper photographs that are different shades of grey as well as black and white.
- Finding dark grey, and light grey in a photograph.
- Making grey.
- Cleaning your fingers and the table top.

Doing

- Choose some squares of paper that are different shades of black, different shades of white and different shades of grey.
- Arrange them on a piece of paper putting the white pieces on one side, the black pieces on the other, and the greys in the middle.
- On a new piece of grey sugar paper, draw and fill in a black shape using either charcoal or a black chalk pastel.
- Near this shape draw and fill another shape, this time using white chalk, or white chalk pastel.
- Use a paper towel or your finger tips to rub part of the black shape and part of the white shape together. You should now have black, white and grey on your paper.
- Now try making different shades of grey. First try making some light greys using lots of white and only a little black.
- Make some dark greys using black and only a little white.
- You will now need to wash your hands and wipe the table!
- Collect some more squares of black, white and grey paper and a new piece of background paper.
- Arrange your squares in a dark to light line across the middle of your page before sticking them down carefully.
- Try and copy this dark to light line underneath, using chalk and charcoal or chalk pastel.

Developing the Idea

- Draw some large shapes on a new piece of paper. Make the centre of each shape very dark, the outside white and the in-between part grey. What does it make you think of? You should have made a tunnel effect.
- Draw some more large shapes. Make these shapes light down one side, dark at the bottom and up the other side, and grey in the middle. What does it make you think of? You should have made a sunshine and shadow effect.
- Make a tonal line using a pencil-remember there is no white to add. How can grey be made? Try pressing firmly and gently.
- Cut and stick part of a black, white and grey newspaper photograph on a new piece of paper. Try to match the different tones next to them.You may be able to hide the piece of photograph if you can make an exact match.

Links with AT2 (Knowledge & Understanding of Other Artists)

Black and white photographs.
Picasso (Guernica).
African Masks.
Rembrandt

Drawing

Session Four.

Activity Extending smudging, pressing and blending.

Focus Tone, colour, line and shape.

Equipment Needed Grey sugar paper A3 and A4 plus strips of the same paper. Charcoal, coloured chalks and chalk pastels, wax crayons felt tip pens, biros and drawing pencils (4B-6B).

Talk About

- What is smudging and how to smudge with finger tips, and how to smudge using a paper towel.
- Drawing media that will smudge.
- Drawing media that will not smudge.
- Naming the media.
- Cleaning your fingers and the table top.
- Pressing down firmly - what happens?
- Pressing down gently - what happens?

Doing

- Ask one child to make some marks on a large piece of paper using a wax crayon and pressing on firmly. The rest of the class keep their eyes closed whilst the marks are drawn, they then guess whether they are firm marks or gentle marks. Repeat this several times.
- Now ask the children to choose a coloured crayon and on their own paper to make a row of firm marks followed by a row of the same marks made by pressing on gently.
- Add more rows of different marks, one row that is firm and the second row that is gentle each time.
- Choose a new piece of paper and use these firm and gentle marks to make a pattern.
- Use a piece of charcoal to draw a thick line across the middle of a new piece of paper. Now put your finger tips on this line and smudge it upwards then downwards. Talk about what happens.
- Cover a new paper with lots of different lines and their smudges. Repeat using coloured chalk or chalk pastels.
- Take a wax crayon and begin colouring at one end of a strip of paper working towards the middle. Stop before you reach the middle. Choose a different coloured crayon and do the same from the other side. The gap in the middle needs to be filled with both colours meeting and blending together. A bit of each will be seen when they first meet but a new colour may appear when they blend together totally.
- Make a multi-coloured snake next that has lots of blends, and pure colours in it.
- Now try a multi -coloured blended line using chalk pastels.

Developing the Idea

- Make a class or group multi-coloured line or snake.
- Make a line or snake that blends from dark to light by both pressing and blending.
- Make blends using the colours found in an artist's painting.
- Make blends or smudges of the colours in a snowy picture.
- Make blends or smudges of the colours seen in a picture of a sunset.

Links with AT2 (Knowledge & Understanding of Other Artists)

W.M.Turner.
Claude Monet.
Edgar Degas.

Drawing

Session Five.

Activity Overdrawing - adding detail afterwards.

Focus Line, shape, colour, pattern and texture.

Equipment Needed Chalk, chalk pastels, charcoal, oil pastel, felt tip pens, A3 and A4 grey sugar paper and Newsprint or Free Art paper 80 gsm

---

Talk About

- Smudging colours and shapes.
- Using the same tool in different ways, e.g.for lines, patterns, shapes and smudges.
- Pressing firmly and pressing gently.
- Working from the top down to avoid unwanted smudging.
- Resting your hand on a scrap piece of paper when working, to avoid unwanted smudging.
- Moving the scrap paper as the drawing progresses.

Doing

- Explore overdrawing i.e. adding detail to a coloured picture you have cut from a magazine using felt pens and oil pastels.
- Choose a new piece of paper and with chalk pastel, cover the paper with blends, patches and smudges of white, blue and green. This is the background on which you are now going to draw still using the chalk pastel but instead of smudges etc. you will be drawing lines, shapes and patterns.
- Before you start, rest a piece of scrap paper under your hand to prevent further smudging.
- On a new piece of paper smudge greens, browns ,yellows and white. Overdraw in lines and shapes something you imagine might live there.
- On your next piece of paper smudge a large shape any colour or even multicoloured. Draw on it and round it to change it into something. Talk about what it has become.
- Now try smudging a row of similar shapes; overdraw and turn them into e.g. a row of houses, or faces. Think carefully about what you will need to add by drawing.

Developing the Idea

- Paint or smudge the shape of a fruit or vegetable. Draw in the details, pattern, texture adding extra colours using other drawing media.
- Make a quick pencil sketch of part of the school building.
- Focus on large shapes only, no detail.
- Paint these shapes on a new piece of paper. Overdraw and add details e.g. brick patterns, using oil pastel or felt tip pens.
- Try a portrait of your friend the same way.

Links with AT2 (Knowledge & Understanding of Other Artists)

W.M.Turner.
John Piper.
Book Illustrations by Brian Wildsmith.

Drawing

Session Six.

Activity Sequencing and storytelling.

Focus Line, shape, pattern and texture.

Equipment Needed A3 size paper either Newsprint or Free Art 80 gsm, Drawing pencils(4B-6B), Black biros or thin black felt tip pens.

Talk About

- Picture only stories in books for non-readers.
- The sequence in a story.
- The repetition of characters, settings etc.
- Comic strip stories-what changes are made to tell the story, e.g facial expressions, weather etc?
- Simple setting out and an easy to follow plot.

Doing

- As a class or group exercise draw together the sequence of a familiar story. Use a large sheet of paper divided into six boxes. Each child takes a turn to draw in a box part of the story, remembering to keep the sequence in order.
- Now ask children to draw their own version of another familiar story in six frames on their own piece of paper.
- Next, the children could draw a six frame picture story about themselves, e.g. my birthday, a day at school etc.
- Ask another child to retell the story to the class, using each picture in turn.
- Finally, draw a story about an imaginary character, to be visually shared and read by the rest of the class.

Developing the Idea

- One child draws part of a story for another child to complete.
- All the children draw a new picture story about the same character e.g.The B.F.G.
- Tell a familiar story but change the ending.
- Draw a story sequence on how to get to the headteacher's office.
- Draw a story sequence on how to play a game.
- Draw a story sequence using an artist's picture as a starting point, e.g. what happened next?

Links with AT2 (Knowledge & Understanding of Other Artists)

Comics.
Picture story books.
Pop Art e.g. Roy Lichenstein.

Materials

Newsprint or Free art paper 80 gsm
Black sugar paper
Grey sugar paper
Black felt tip pens (thick and thin)
Coloured felt tip pens (thick and thin)
Wax crayons
Oil pastels
Charcoal
Chalk
Drawing pencils (4B - 6B)
Paint brushes (thick and thin)
Powder paint or ready mix paint
Palettes/Inking trays
Glue
Glue spreaders
Biros
Sequins
Coloured buttons
Chalk pastels

Suppliers

NES Arnold Ltd
Ludlow Hill Road
West Bridgeford
NOTTINGHAM
NG2 6HD

Pisces
Westwood Studies
West Avenue
CREWE
Cheshire
CW1 3AD

Philip & Tracey Ltd
North Way
Andover
Hampshire
SP10 5BA

Hope Education
Orb Mill
Huddersfield Road
OLDHAM
Lancashire
OL4 2ST

Yorkshire Purchasing Organisation
41 Industrial Park
WAKEFIELD
WF2 0XE

Drawing

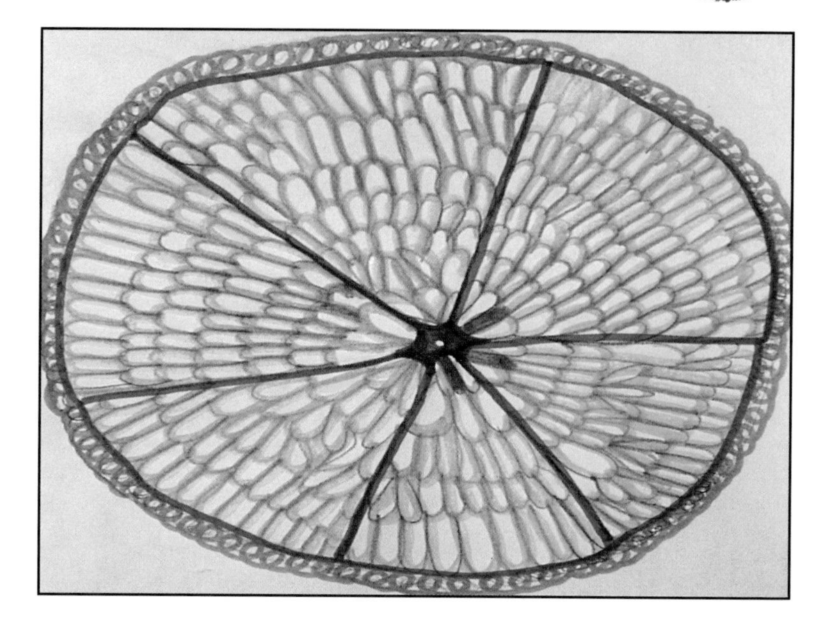

Session 1
Example of using line patterns in observational drawing.

Session 2
Example of exploring shape by adding lines.

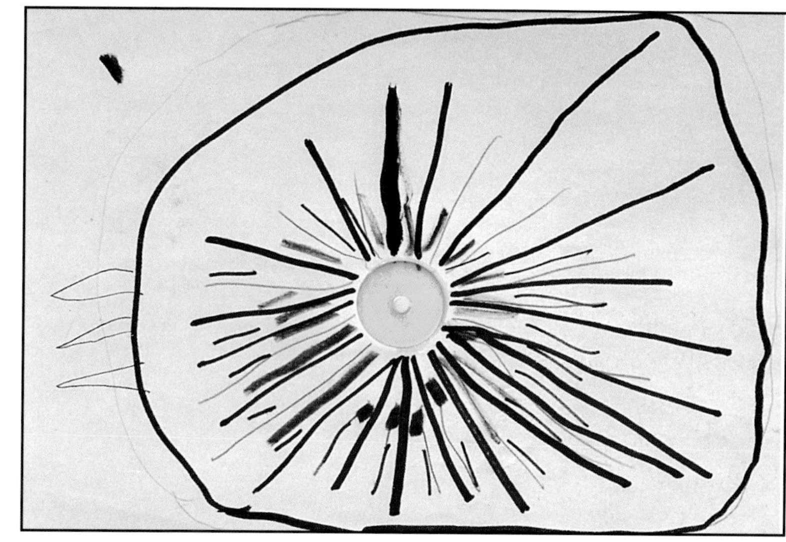

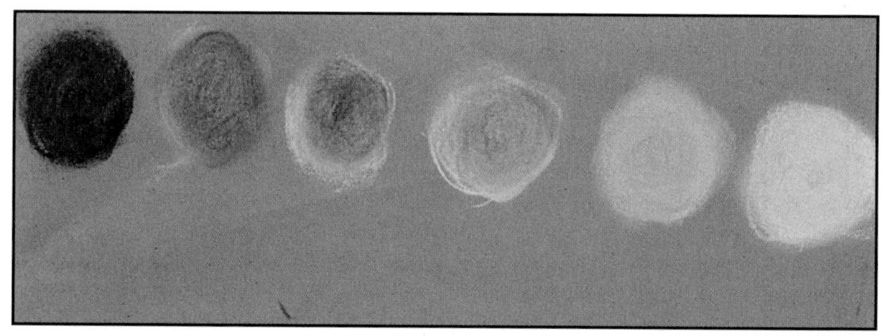

Session 3
Example of finding and making light and dark.

Drawing

Session 4
Example of smudging, pressing, and blending.

Session 5
Example of overdrawing.

How to get to Mr Green's office from class 1C.

1. you get to a step you go down it then go past some coats.
2. Then you turn right and go through some doors.
3. Then you go past 2p walk straight on then go past Mrs Ruddocks.
4. Then turn left and go through a door.
5. past toys turn right down steps through
6. Straight on turn left.

Session 6
Example of sequencing and storytelling.

Painting

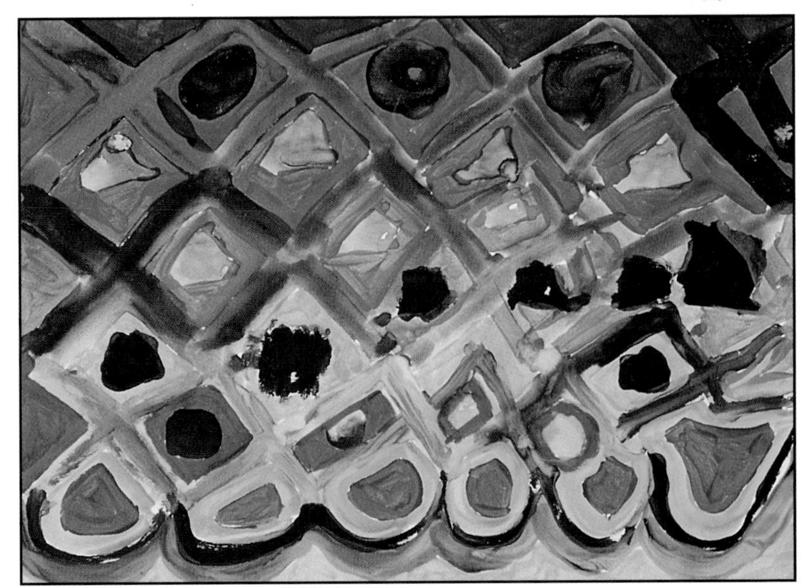

Session 1
Example of a pattern using dark shades only.

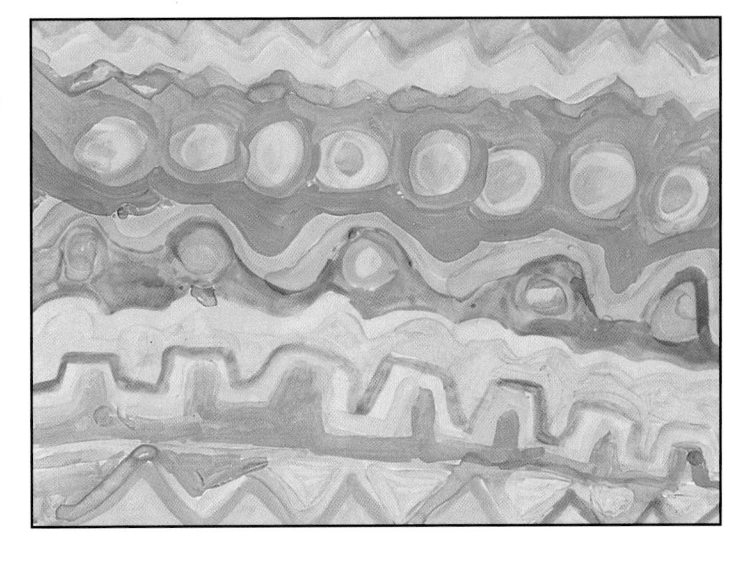

Session 2
Example of a pattern using light shades only.

Session 3
Example of a pattern using light and dark shades on coloured paper.

Painting

Session 4
Example of making brown.

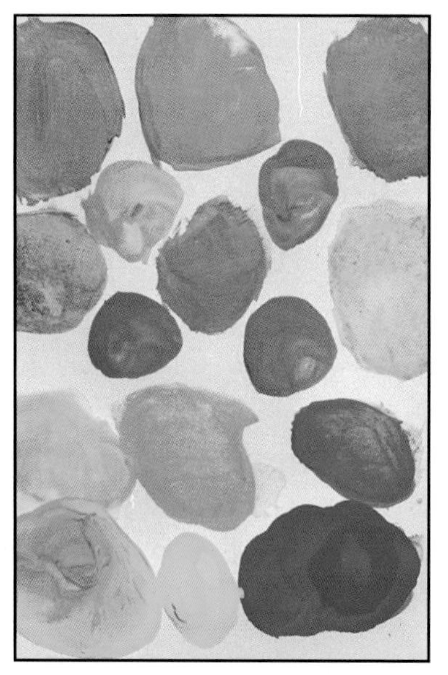

Session 5
Example of working with a colour family.

Session 6
Example of using thick and thin paint.

Painting

Painting

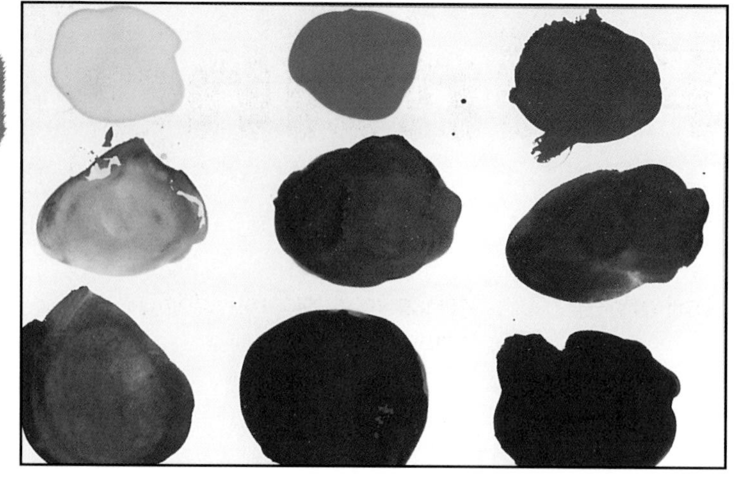

Session One.

Activity Colour, pattern.

Focus Making dark colours - adding black.

Equipment Needed Card pieces to be used as mixing palettes, thick and thin brushes, A3 Newsprint or Free Art 80 gsm, A3 paper in both dark and light colours, black, red, yellow and blue ready mix, or powder paint water pots and paper towels.

Talk About

- Collecting objects from the classroom that are differing shades of the same colour.
- Descriptions or names for the different shades.
- Sorting the darkest shades into a new group.
- Making colours darker by adding black.
- The need to use very little black, or else colour disappears.
- Making more than one dark shade.

Doing

- Choose either red, blue or yellow paint and put several blobs of it on your card palette.
- Put only one small blob of black on your palette.
- Choose a thick or a thin brush.
- Use your brush to add a little black to one blob of colour, a little more to the next one, and repeat until each coloured blob has its share of black.
- Mix each coloured blob and its black together using your brush .
- Talk about the dark shades you have made and whether they are all the same, or slightly different.
- Put several blobs of red, yellow and blue, on a new card palette and one small blob of black.
- Try adding a little, and then more black to each coloured blob, and mix them together.
- You should have made darker shades of all your colours.
- Talk about them and compare them to those your friends have made.

Developing the Idea

- Paint a pattern using dark shades only.
- Paint a picture using dark shades only.
- Paint dark shades on dark coloured paper and discuss.
- Paint dark shades on pale coloured paper and discuss.
- Look at the work of artists that have used dark colours. How do they make you feel? Why do you think the artist has used dark colours?

Links with AT2 (Knowledge & Understanding of Other Artists)

L.S.Lowry.
Rembrandt.
Mark Rothko.

Painting

Session Two.

Activity Making light colours - adding white.

Focus Colour, pattern.

Equipment Needed Card pieces as mixing palettes, thick and thin brushes, A3 Newsprint or Free Art 80gsm, A3 dark and light coloured paper, red, yellow, blue, and white ready mix or powder paint. Thick and thin brushes.

Talk About

- Collecting objects from the classroom that are differing shades of the same colour.
- Names or descriptions for the different shades.
- Sorting the lightest shades into a new group.
- Making colours lighter by adding white.
- Adding colour to white and not the other way around.
- Making more than one light shade.

Doing

- Put several blobs of white paint on your card palette, and one blob only, of either red, yellow, or blue paint.
- Use your brush to add a little colour to one blob of white, slightly more to the next one, and repeat until each white blob has its share of colour.
- Mix each white blob and its colour together using your brush.
- Talk about the light shades you have made and whether they are all the same.
- Put a small blob of each primary colour, plus several blobs of white, on a new card palette.
- Add colour to each of the blobs of white, and mix in with your brush. You should have made paler shades of all your colours.
- Talk about them, and compare them with the shades your friends have made.

Developing the Idea

- Paint a pattern using light shades only.
- Paint a picture using light shades only.
- Paint light shades on dark coloured paper and discuss.
- Paint light shades on light coloured paper and discuss.
- Look at the work of artists that have used mainly light shades. How do they make you feel? Why do you think the artist has used light colours?

Links with AT2 (Knowledge & Understanding of Other Artists)

Elizabeth Blackadder.
Beatrix Potter.
Charles Rennie Mackintosh (paintings).

Painting

Session Three.

Activity Using light and dark colours together.

Focus Colour and pattern.

Equipment Needed A3 Newsprint or Free Art 80 gsm. A3 pale and dark papers. Red, blue, yellow, black and white paint-ready mix or powder colour. Thick and thin brushes, and pieces of card to use as palettes.

Talk About

- Objects collected from the classroom that are different shades of the same colour. Sorting the objects into groups; light colours and dark colours.
- Collecting a different colour group and adding those lights and darks to the first group.
- Finding specific colours e.g. an object that is dark red or light blue etc.
- Recap on adding black sparingly to darken a colour.
- Recap on adding small amounts of colour to white to make light colours.

Doing

- Choose one primary colour plus black and white, and either a thick or thin brush.
- Put a large blob of your colour in the middle of a card palette.
- Spread it into a large shape using your brush.
- Put several blobs of white down one side of your shape, near it but not touching.
- Use your brush to mix the colour with each blob of white.
- You should have made several pale shades of your colour.
- Put several very small blobs of black down the other side of your shape, near but not touching.
- Use a clean brush, mix the colour with each blob of black.
- You should have made several dark shades of your colour.
- Your palette should have pure colour on it surrounded by dark shades and light shades.

Developing the Idea

- Use all the primary colours plus black and white in the same way and on the same card palette.
- Paint a pattern of light and dark shapes and light and dark lines.
- Paint a pattern with light and dark colours on pale paper, and then on dark paper. Talk about the difference.
- Paint a line or a pattern that starts with light colours and gradually gets darker.
- Look at the work of artists that use lights and darks of the same colour. Find the different shades and talk about them.

Links with AT2 (Knowledge & Understanding of Other Artists)

Henri Rousseau - Jungle pictures.
Claude Monet - Bridge over the lily pond.
Georges Seurat.

Painting

Session Four.

Activity Making and naming colours of your own, including brown.

Focus Colour.

Equipment Needed Card pieces to use as palettes, thick and thin brushes, the primary colours plus black and white readymix or powder paint, water pots, paper towels, A3 and A4 size paper Newsprint or Free Art 80 gsm.

Talk About

- The names of each of the primary colours.
- The new colour that each pair of primary colours make when they are mixed together.
- What all three primary colours might make if they were mixed together.
- Cleaning your brush properly after mixing a colour and going on to the next.
- Using water to clean a brush, or water then a paper towel to give it a better clean.

Doing

- Put a blob of each primary colour on a card palette and choose either a thick or thin brush.
- Mix all three colours together and describe what they have made.
- Now make three blobs of brown on your palette.
- Add a little more red to one, more blue to another and more yellow to the last.
- How has your brown changed? How else could your brown be changed? Remember adding black and white before?
- Make two more blobs of brown on your palette and try adding a little black to one, then add a little of your other brown to the white. You should now have made lots of different browns.
- On a new palette put a blob of two or three colours that you would like to mix together. You can include black and white in your choice. Mix these two or three colours together.
- Describe the new colour you have made.
- Now try more two or three colour mixes. Stop when you have made five new colours of your own.
- Give each one a name and describe how you made it.

Developing the Idea

- Make a class collection of all the new colours and their names plus descriptions of how to make them.
- Paint a picture or a pattern using your own new colours.
- Find an artist's painting that has similar colours in it to the ones you have made. Discuss who it is by and what is it called?
- Make a class collection of all the browns made.
- Make a list of their names and what they remind you of.
- Make a collection of objects that match the shades of brown.

Links with AT2 (Knowledge & Understanding of Other Artists)

Raoul Dufy.
Andre Derain.
Marc Chagall.

Painting

Session Five.

Activity Working with a colour family.

Focus Colour, pattern.

Equipment Needed Primary colours of readymix or powder paint plus black and white. A3 Newsprint or Free Art 80 gsm, card to use as palettes, thick and thin brushes, glue and glue spreaders, magazines, assorted coloured paper, paper plates or squares of card.

Talk About

- What makes a family?
- What makes a colour family?
- Finding and collecting objects that belong to a colour family.
- Finding and collecting papers that belong to the same colour family.
- Arranging and then sticking a paper colour family on a paper plate or square of card.
- Where to put the glue and how much to use.

Doing

- Choose a collection of papers that belong to the same colour family.
- Cut or tear them into small shapes and strips.
- Arrange and then stick them on your paper plate, or card square to cover the whole surface.
- Group all the class colour families that match together.
- Now choose a new piece of paper, a card palette and either a thick or thin brush.
- Put blobs of two primary colours on your palette, close but not touching.
- You are going to mix some of each colour together to make a new colour. Try and make this new colour slightly different each time, by using sometimes more, and sometimes less of the colour you started with. Remember it must belong and match the same colour family, and not change into a totally new colour. Add a little black and white as well to add more colours to your colour family.
- Paint some stripes or shapes on your paper using all your new colours.

Developing the Idea

- Try making more colour families using the other primary colours in pairs.
- Make a class or group colour family - each child working individually with the same starting colours, plus black and white. The colours to be used to paint a group or class pattern based on the same shapes, e.g. squares.
- Collect magazine pictures and paper pieces that belong to a colour family.
- Tear them into strips and stick them on an A3 piece of paper, leaving gaps between them.
- Fill the gaps with colours you have mixed, that belong to the same colour family.

Links with AT2 (Knowledge & Understanding of Other Artists)

Paul Klee -The Rose Garden.
Vincent van Gogh- Sunflowers.
Henri Rousseau-Jungle pictures.

Painting

Session Six.

Activity Using thick and thin paint.

Focus Texture.

Equipment Needed Primary colours of readymix or powder paint, thick and thin brushes, glue spreaders, A3 Newsprint or Free Art 80 gsm, PVA glue, plastic palettes or inking trays.

Talk About

- The brush strokes you can see in an artist's painting, and why they can be seen easily.
- An artist's painting in which the brush strokes cannot be seen, and why.
- Either -How to mix thick powder paint, or how to make readymix paint thicker by adding some PVA.
- Using a glue spreader, or old brush if there is glue in the paint.
- And how to make readymix and powder paint thinner by adding water.

Doing

- Mix some thin paint in a plastic palette or inking tray.
- Choose a brush and a piece of A3 paper.
- Paint a stripe across your page at the top.
- Lift your paper gently, and watch the paint run downwards.
- Put the paper down flat, turn it and paint a stripe of thin paint along a second edge. Lift your paper gently and watch the paint run downwards again. Repeat along the remaining two edges.
- Try this with thick paint and talk about the difference. How can you get the thick paint to spread? Try your idea out.
- Drop some thin paint from your brush on to a new piece of paper that you have first painted with water, and watch it spread.
- Try dropping some other colours of thin paint on the same paper. Watch what happens when the colours meet and merge. Leave the paper flat to dry.
- Mix some thick paint, and use a glue spreader to scoop some of it on to a new piece of paper.
- Use the glue spreader to explore spreading the paint, drawing different marks in the paint and merging different colours of thick paint together.

Developing the Idea

- When you have run thin paint down the edge of a piece of paper, try running a second colour on top before the first one dries. Again repeat it on each edge. When the paint has dried use other colours to fill in the spaces.
- Blob a colour family onto a wet piece of paper.
- Blob each of the primary colours onto a wet piece of paper.
- Cover your paper with different colours of thin paint. Leave it to dry. Use thick paint to draw or make a pattern on top of the thin paint.
- Look at the marks in part of a Van Gogh picture. Copy some of the marks and use them in a picture of your own.

Links with AT2 (Knowledge & Understanding of Other Artists)

Vincent van Gogh.
Gustav Klimt-Landscapes.
Pierre Bonnard.
Watercolour paintings.

Materials

Paint brushes (thick and thin)
Ready mix paint or powder paint
Palettes/Inking trays
Water pots

Newsprint or Free art paper 80 gsm
Sugar paper (assorted colours)

Suppliers

NES Arnold Ltd
Ludlow Hill Road
West Bridgeford
NOTTINGHAM
NG2 6HD

Pisces
Westwood Studies
West Avenue
CREWE
Cheshire
CW1 3AD

Philip & Tracey Ltd
North Way
Andover
Hampshire
SP10 5BA

Hope Education
Orb Mill
Huddersfield Road
OLDHAM
Lancashire
OL4 2ST

Yorkshire Purchasing Organisation
41 Industrial Park
WAKEFIELD
WF2 0XE

Printing

Printing

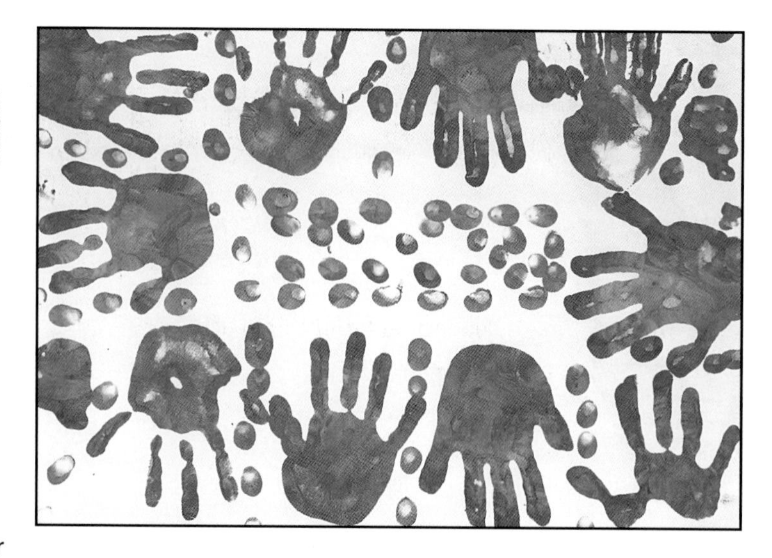

Session One.

Activity Exploring hand prints.

Focus Shape, pattern and colour.

Equipment Needed Inking trays, paper towels, Readymix paint, A3 Newsprint or Free Art 80 gsm.

Talk About

- Putting your hand flat in a tray of Readymix paint.
- How to print using you hand by pressing on then taking it off the paper.
- Making several prints before putting your hand back in the tray for more paint.
- Using your other hand for a second colour.
- Rubbing your hands together to colour mix and make a new colour to print with.
- Printing with the new colour.
- Wiping your hands on a paper towel afterwards.

Doing

- Press one hand in a tray of paint, then press it on to a piece of paper several times in different places.
- Press your other hand in a tray of paint that is a different colour, and print with it on the same paper again in several different places.
- Some of the prints may touch the first ones and even go on top of them.
- Put each hand in its own colour of paint again.
- Rub your hands together before you print again.
- You have now made a new colour to print with.
- Return to your paper and print several times in different places, including next to and on top of your other hand prints.
- Wipe your hands clean on a paper towel.

Developing the Idea

- Print on different colours of paper.
- Make a collaborative class hand prints pattern on a large sheet of paper.
- Print hands round in a circle.
- Print hands in a line with each one pointing upwards and then a line with each one pointing downwards.
- Print hands in a group in the middle of your paper, leave a space and print other hand prints around the edge as a border.
- Make a new hand print pattern of your own.

Links with AT2 (Knowledge & Understanding of Other Artists)

Richard Long.
Wrapping paper designs.
Wallpaper and textile designs.

Printing

Session Two.

Activity Extending hand prints and finger prints.

Focus Shape, pattern.

Equipment Needed One colour only of readymix paint, inking trays, paper towels A3 Newsprint or Free Art 80gsm.

Talk About

- Using only one colour of paint.
- Making different marks by printing with other parts of your hand.
- Which parts of your hand to try printing with.
- What each part is called.
- Pressing one part at a time into the paint and printing with it before trying the next part.
- Wiping your hands in between using each part.

Doing

- Dip the tip of your finger in paint and print with it on a piece of paper several times.
- Wipe it clean.
- Now try printing with your knuckle.
- Clean your hand, then try printing with the side of your hand.
- Next wipe your hand and try printing with the bottom of your palm.
- Look at and talk about the prints you have made. Are they all the same?
- Which ones were easy to make and which ones were difficult?
- Think of another part of your hand to use and try printing with it.
- On a fresh piece of paper, print a row of each different mark you have made.

Developing the Idea

- Print a pattern using one colour of paint and several different parts of your hand. Use a second colour and add more prints on, between, next to and above the first prints.
- Now try a three colour pattern. Remember to wipe your hand between each new colour.
- Try printing a pattern on a round piece of paper - look at the shape before you start printing and let it influence where the printing goes.
- Use whole hand prints as well as different parts of your hand to print a pattern.
- Print on different colours of paper.

Links with AT2 (Knowledge & Understanding of Other Artists)

Aboriginal art.
Richard Long.
Textile and wallpaper design.

Printing

Session Three

Activity Vegetable prints.

Focus Shape and pattern.

Equipment Needed Potatoes cut into different shapes for printing, inking trays, ready mix paint, A3 size Newsprint or Free Art 80 gsm paper, paint brushes.

Talk About

- The shapes of the potato blocks.
- How to hold them and dip them in paint.
- How to print with them by pressing them on and taking them off the paper.
- How often to return and add more paint.
- How to put paint on a potato block with a brush -and then print.
- Other vegetable and fruit blocks for printing.

Doing

- Choose a potato shape and dip it in one colour of paint, before pressing it on a piece of paper to print.
- Choose other potato shapes, use the same colour paint each time and explore the shapes these will print on the same piece of paper.
- Now choose two shapes to use to print a pattern on a new piece of paper.
- Print one row of one shape, then one row of the other using the same colour paint as before. Repeat the pattern again all the way down your paper.
- Now print a new pattern on another piece of paper using the same colour paint and the same shapes but alternate the shapes.

Developing the Idea

- Print a pattern using two colours of paint - one for each shape.
- Print a dark to light pattern using two colours, and two shapes but only applying paint at the beginning of each row. Use each shape in turn to print a complete row.
- Print a series of circles with one shape in one colour, leaving a space in the middle of each circle. Use a second shape and a second colour, to print in the middle of each circle.
- Print a row of shapes in one colour, then overprint in a second colour with a different shape.
- Invent a pattern of your own.
- Explore printing and making patterns using other fruit and vegetables. Try each one on its own first before printing a pattern using several different vegetables together.

Links with AT2 (Knowledge & Understanding of Other Artists)

Wrapping paper designs.
Wallpaper designs.
Patterns on the edge of book pages.

Printing

Session Four.

Activity Making a printing block.

Focus Shape and pattern.

Equipment Needed Readymix paint, inking trays, plasticene, paint brushes, A3 Newsprint or Free Art 80 gsm, paper towels.

Talk About

- Making small shapes with the plasticene.
- Making sure the shapes are fairly thick and easy to hold.
- How to hold a shape and dip it in the paint.
- Alternatively how to put paint on the plasticene block using a brush.
- How to print with the plasticene, remembering not to press on too hard, because it will change the shape of the block.
- Using only one colour of paint to begin with.

Doing

- Make a small, thick plasticene shape to print with.
- Dip it carefully in the paint or put paint on it with a brush.
- Press the shape carefully on your piece of paper, and look at the shape your printing block has made.
- Change your plasticene shape if you want to alter your print, or if you do not like the shape it has printed. Wipe your block on a paper towel first.
- Make several more plasticene blocks.
- Print with each one in turn to see the shapes they print.
- Choose two of your shapes to print a pattern. Use a different colour for each shape and print each shape on alternate rows.
- Now try a pattern using the same shapes and two colours but alternating the shapes.

Developing the Idea

- Explore printing on different colours of paper.
- Print a pattern on a square, triangular or circular piece of paper. Let the shape of the paper act as a guide for the pattern and where the printing goes.
- Make a class combined print using everyones plasticene shapes and lots of colours.
- Make a plasticene shape from observation e.g. a leaf shape and use it to print a pattern.

Links with AT2 (Knowledge & Understanding of Other Artists)

Wrapping paper.
Tea towels.
Textiles whose patterns show repeating shapes.

Printing

Session Five.

Activity Making a different printing block.

Focus Shape and pattern.

Equipment Needed Readymix paint, inking trays, paint brushes, scissors, rolls of draught excluder (the foam self-adhesive sort from a D.I.Y. store), empty margarine tubs and aerosol lids, paper towels, A3 Newsprint or Free Art 80 gsm.

Talk About

- The draught excluder that will be used for printing.
- How to cut it in strips, and stick it on the base of an aerosol lid or margarine tub.
- Cutting and arranging several strips that may touch but not overlap, to make a design.
- How to hold the block and dip it in the paint, or how to put the paint on the block using a brush.
- How to print with the block.

Doing

- Choose a lid, or margarine tub, a pair of scissors, and a strip of draught excluder.
- Cut a piece of draught excluder from your strip and press it on to the bottom of your lid or margarine tub. As it is self - adhesive it should stick easily.
- Cut some more pieces from your strip and stick them on as well.You have now made a printing block with a design on it.
- The block needs some paint on it, then it will be ready to print with.
- Dip the block in some paint or put paint on it using a brush, and press your block on to a piece of paper.
- If you are pleased with your design, print with it several more times and make a pattern. If you do not like it, wipe your block on a paper towel, and move some of the strips around, or take some off or stick some more on. Add more paint and print again.
- Print a row of your new design when you are happy with it.
- Wipe your block on a paper towel and print a second row in a different colour.

Developing the Idea

- Make a second printing block that is different from the first.
- Use them both together to print a pattern. Use a different colour for each block. Try alternating the rows or alternating the blocks each time.
- Try printing the designs on top of one another, or printing circles in one design and using the other to print in the centre of each circle.
- Stick a group of shapes e.g. flower shapes on the same lid and paint on several different colours before you print with it.
- Print on different colours of paper.

Links with AT2 (Knowledge & Understanding of Other Artists)

Indian wood blocks.
Book Illustrations using wood block or lino block prints.

Printing

Session Six.

Activity Taking drawing into printing.

Focus Line and shape.

Equipment Needed Pressprint or Easiprint tiles cut into quarters to make them go further, pencils, scissors, inking trays, water-based printing ink (one colour only), printing ink rollers, magazines, A4 coloured paper, A4 Newsprint or Free Art 80 gsm.

Talk About

- The tools and materials that are going to be used.
- How they are going to be used.
- Pressing in firmly with a pencil when drawing into the Pressprint.
- Making different sorts of marks.
- How to use a roller in an inking tray and how to roll ink on to a Pressprint tile.
- How to print the drawing on paper.
- Keeping the inking area clean by working on an open magazine when inking a tile. After inking and printing, remembering to turn over a page to leave a clean working area for the next person.

Doing

- Choose a piece of Pressprint and a pencil.
- Draw a pattern, or picture, or shapes on your tile, remembering to press in firmly all the time.
- Use different lines and dots to decorate your pattern, picture or shape.
- Now put your tile on the clean, open magazine next to the inking tray.
- Push the roller up and down the inking tray several times to cover it with ink. Then roll it across your drawing on the tile.
- Make sure it all gets covered. A couple of times should be enough.
- Place a piece of paper on top of your inked up tile and smooth it down all over, pressing down firmly.
- Lift up the paper to see your print.
- Now turn over the magazine page you have used, and the inking area will be left clean and ready for the next person to use.

Developing the Idea

- Print on different colours of paper.
- Print a row of tiles that touch each other.
- Cut a shape, e.g. a fish, out of the Pressprint, decorate it with a pattern, ink it up and print it.
- Print a quantity of, e.g. fish, on a background you have painted.
- Make a group or class print with each child contributing the same motif e.g. a house to a street scene.

Links with AT2 (Knowledge & Understanding of Other Artists)

Wood block book illustrations.
Lino cut book illustrations.
Andy Warhol.

Materials

Ready mix paint
Paint brushes (thick and thin)
Palettes/Inking trays
Water based printing ink
Sponge rollers or rubber rollers

Free Art paper 80 gsm or Newsprint
Sticky paper
Sugar paper (assorted colours)
Scissors
Glue
Glue spreaders
Card (4 sheet thickness)
Plasticene
Press Print or Easiprint or Poly Block
Draught excluder

Suppliers

NES Arnold Ltd
Ludlow Hill Road
West Bridgeford
NOTTINGHAM
NG2 6HD

Pisces
Westwood Studies
West Avenue
CREWE
Cheshire
CW1 3AD

Philip & Tracey Ltd
North Way
Andover
Hampshire
SP10 5BA

Hope Education
Orb Mill
Huddersfield Road
OLDHAM
Lancashire
OL4 2ST

Yorkshire Purchasing Organisation
41 Industrial Park
WAKEFIELD
WF2 0XE

Printing

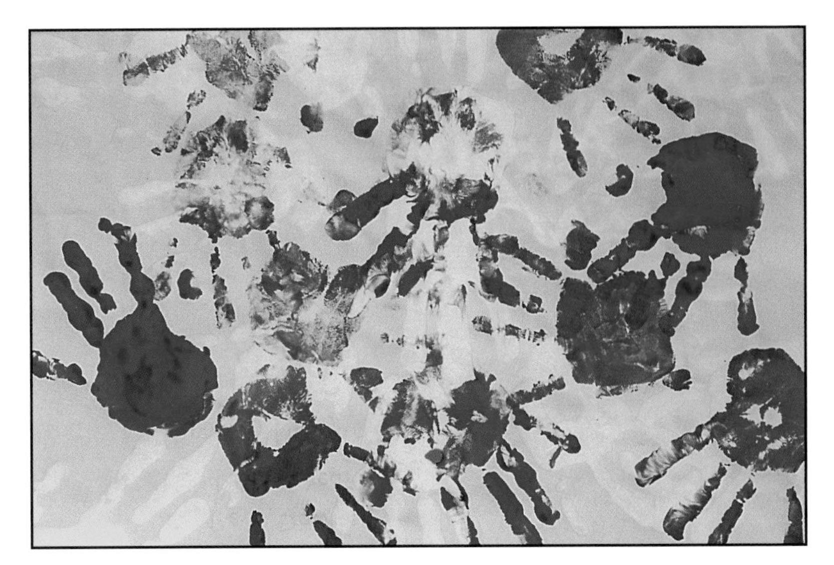

Session 1
Example of exploring hand prints.

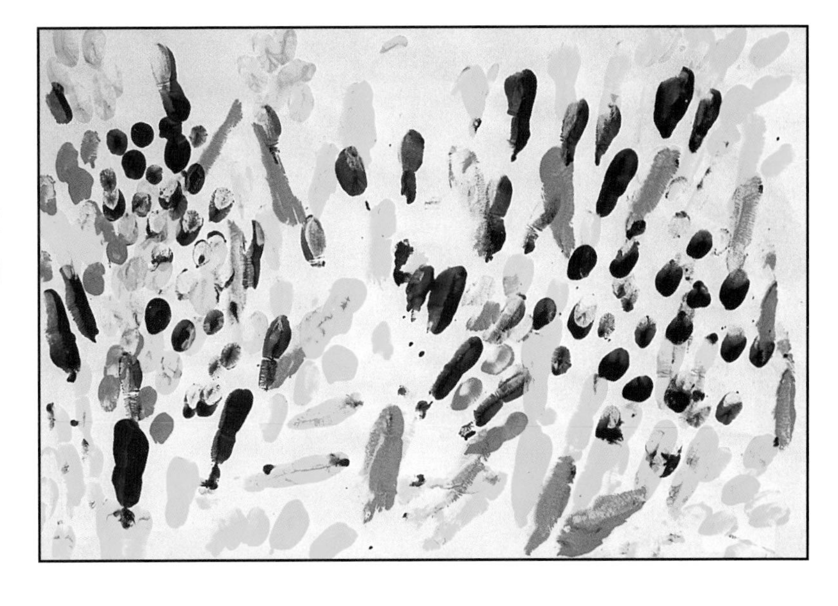

Session 2
Examples of using finger prints.

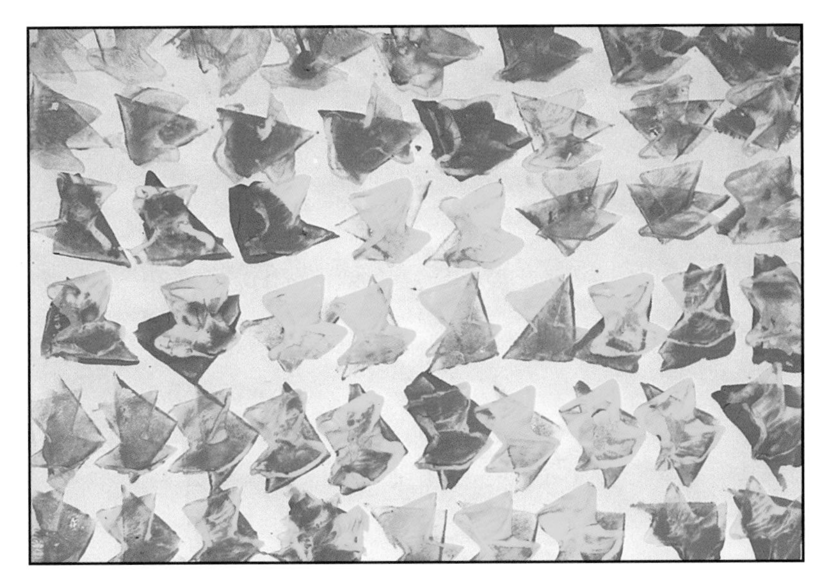

Session 3
Examples of use of vegetable prints.

Printing

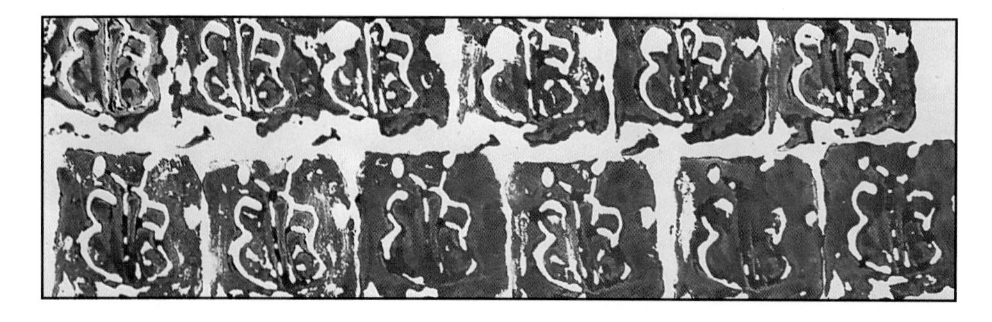

Session 4
Example of using a plasticene printing block.

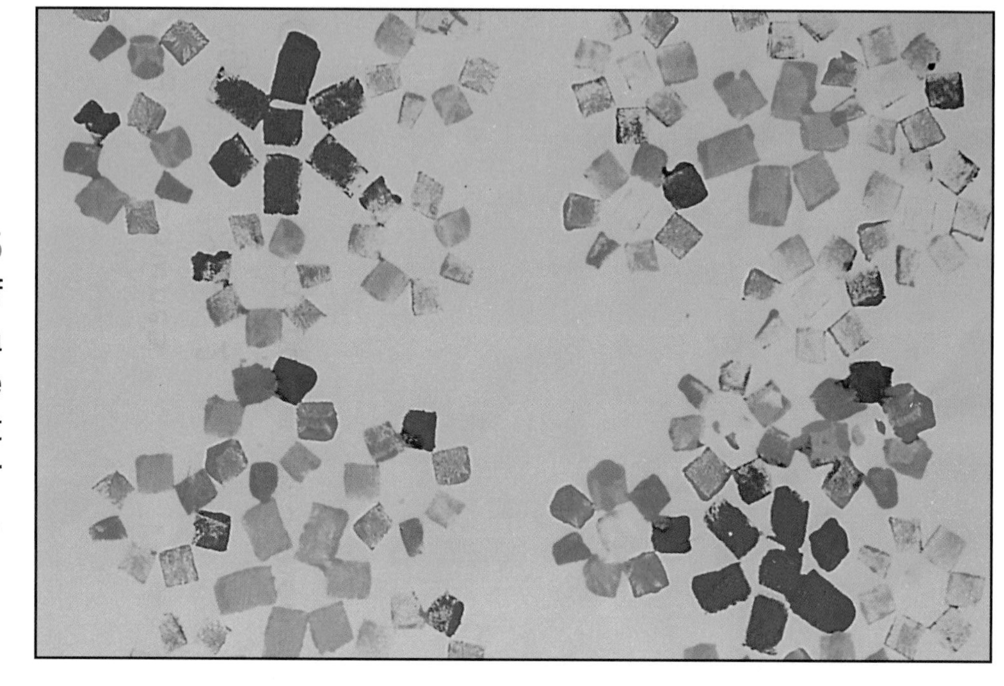

Session 5
Example of making a pattern with the same draught excluder printing block.

Session 6
Example of taking drawing into printing using Press Print.

Collage

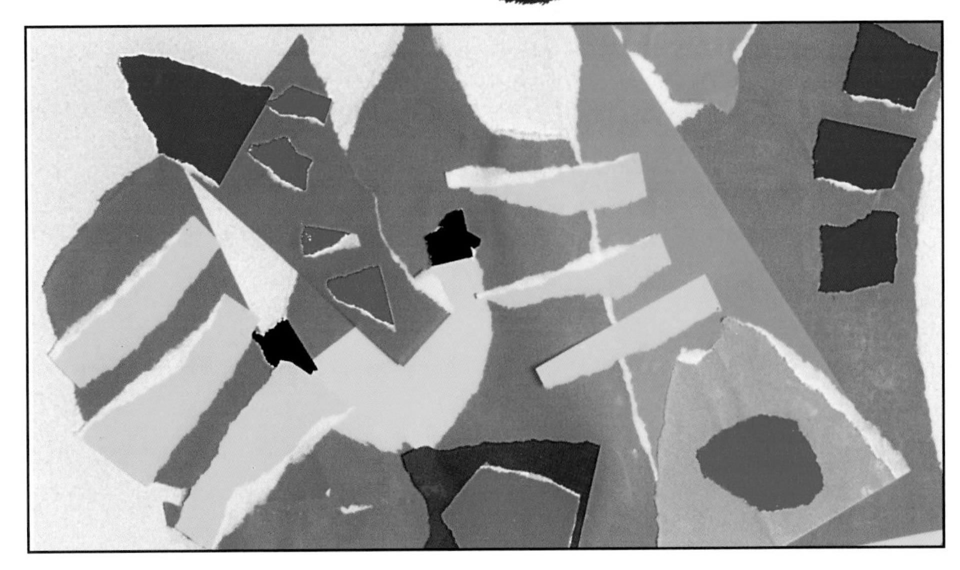

Session 1
Example of making new shapes by tearing, arranging and adding.

Session 2
Example of cutting and arranging shapes.

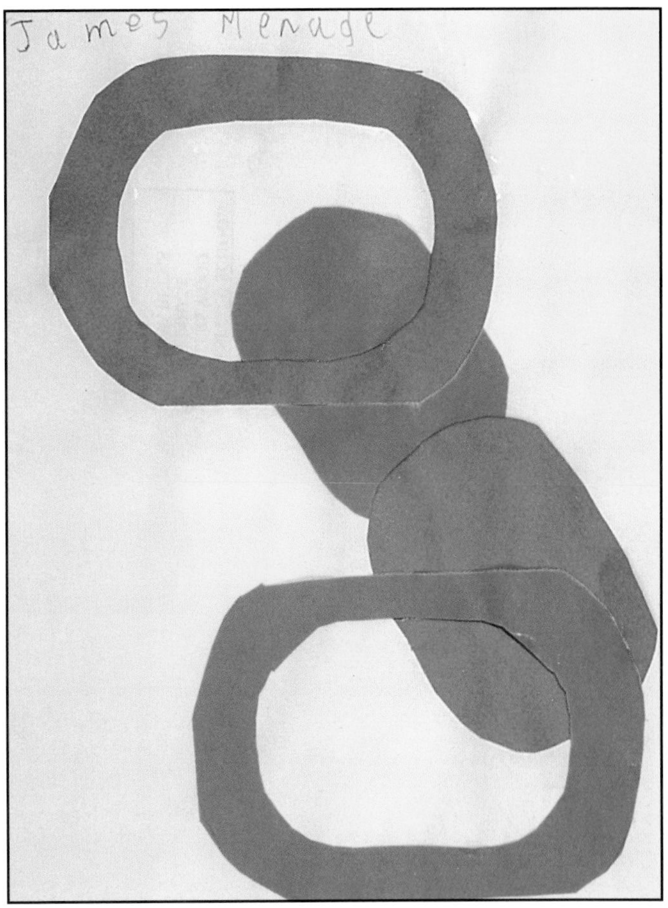

Session 3
Example of folding and cutting strip patterns.

Collage

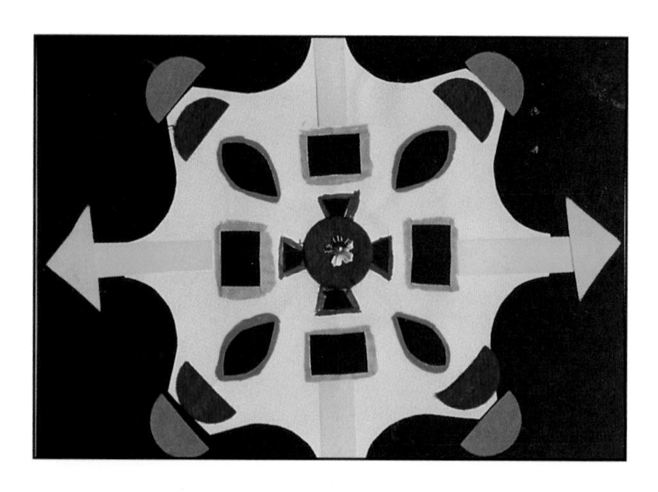

Session 4
Example of cutting and decorating circle patterns.

Session 5
Example of curling, fanning, and twisting.

Session 6
Example of finding, matching and re-arranging shapes and colours based on a Matisse collage.

Collage

Collage

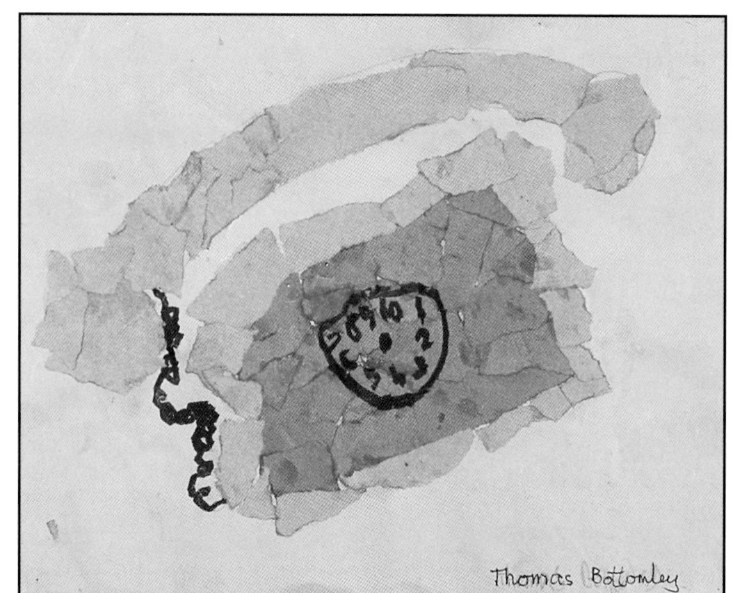

Session

One.

Activity

Making and decorating new shapes by tearing, arranging and adding.

Focus

Colour and shape

Equipment Needed

Coloured papers, glue, gluespreaders, A3 Newsprint or Free Art 80 gsm.

Talk About

- Tearing a group of large and small shapes in one colour only.
- Arranging them close together to make a new shape (no gaps allowed) before sticking them down.
- Where to put the glue and how much to use.
- Tearing shapes from other colours, to add to the first shape that you have made and stuck down.
- Where to stick these extra torn shapes-on, above beside or below the first shape to decorate and change it.

Doing

- Choose a coloured piece of paper and tear a group of different sized shapes from it.
- Now arrange these shapes close together on a piece of paper to make a new shape. Your new shape could be long and thin, round, wavy, spiky etc.
- Describe the new shape you have made.
- You are now going to decorate and add to your new shape with other colours and shapes.
- Look at your shape carefully before you begin and when you have decided what you are going to do, choose the other coloured papers you want to use.
- Tear the shapes you need from your newspapers and arrange them on and around your stuck down shape.
- You may want to try several arrangements before you are satisfied.
- Stick your new shapes down carefully.

Developing the Idea

- Turn your new decorated shape into, e.g. a mini beast, a fish, or a monster by adding some drawing to it as well.
- The whole class focus on the same theme, e.g. faces, and use the same approach to create torn and decorated face collages.
- Make torn and decorated collages from observation, e.g. leaves.
- Each child to make half a torn and decorated face, monster or flower for another child to complete.
- Make a torn shape repeating pattern using both large and small shapes- repeating the colours and shapes carefully.
- Make a cut and decorated shape collage and discuss the difference.

Links with AT2 (Knowledge & Understanding of Other Artists)

Archimboldo.
Braque.
Picasso.

Collage

Session Two.

Activity Folding and cutting shapes and holes.

Focus Shape.

Equipment Needed Coloured papers, scissors, glue, glue spreaders, pencils, lids from margarine tubs, plus other lids of varying shapes and sizes to draw round, News print or Free Art 80 gsm paper.

Talk About

- What is a shape, and what is a hole in a shape.
- Drawing round a shape with a pencil.
- Cutting out the shape by keeping the scissors on the pencil line you have drawn.
- Folding the shape in half.
- Cutting a shape inside the folded shape by starting on the fold and following the edge of the folded shape, but a little way in from start to finish.
- Taking out the smaller cut shape, opening the folded shape and discovering the hole you have cut.
- Arranging and sticking shapes with holes and shapes without holes.
- Where to put the glue and how much to use.

Doing

- Choose a piece of coloured paper, a pencil, and a lid to draw round.
- Hold your lid down on the paper with one hand, whilst you draw round it with your pencil in the other hand.
- Use scissors to cut carefully along the line you have drawn to cut out your shape.
- Cut out some more shapes using different lids and different colours of paper-remember to draw round them carefully first.
- Now fold each of your shapes in half.
- Look at the fold on each shape as this is where you are going to use your scissors next.
- Choose one of your folded shapes, and start cutting a little way up the fold, following the edge but keeping a little way in all round the shape.
- You should end up with two shapes,one with a hole in it and one without.
- Cut your other folded shapes in the same way.
- Choose a new piece of paper and try arranging the shapes in different ways before you stick them down e.g. shapes on top of shapes, shapes inside the holes, overlapping holes etc.

Developing the Idea

- Recut one folded shape several times, making it smaller and smaller. Arrange and stick all the shapes on the same piece of paper.
- Try the same approach but this time draw round square shapes to fold and cut, arranging and sticking them down.
- Make a collage in which you have used round shapes and square shapes, both with holes and without holes.
- Make a class or group shape collage, using squares and circles in lots of different colours, some with holes and some without.
- Make a collage of shapes all of which have holes in them, and cut new shapes of your own to go in the holes.

Links with AT2 (Knowledge & Understanding of Other Artists)

Book Illustrations.
Wrapping paper designs.

Collage

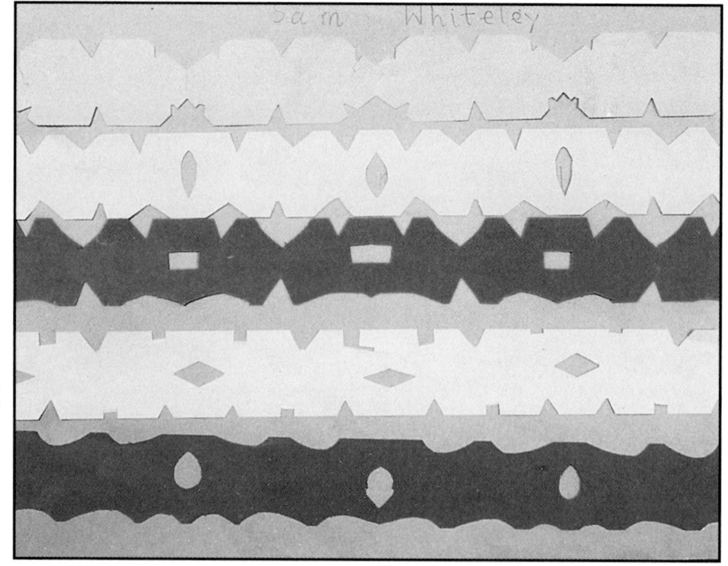

Session Three.

Activity Folding and cutting strip patterns.

Focus Shape and pattern.

Equipment Needed Scissors, glue, glue spreaders, A4 black card or A4 black paper, strips of coloured paper 5 cm width and cut to fit portrait style across the A4 black paper or card.

Talk About

- Folding a paper strip lengthwise once, and then folding it over lengthwise again.
- Where to cut on each edge.
- Leaving the top and bottom of each folded edge intact and still joined together.
- The sort of cuts that could be made e.g. zig-zags, curves etc.
- Opening the strip carefully.
- Looking at and talking about the cut pattern.
- Arranging the strips across a piece of card before sticking them down.
- How much glue to use and where to put it.

Doing

- Choose a strip of coloured paper and a pair of scissors.
- Fold the paper strip in half lengthwise once, then fold it over lengthwise again.
- Use your scissors to cut a shape out of the top edge.
- Next use your scissors to cut the same shape out of the bottom edge.
- Now cut a shape out of the middle of one of the folded edges.
- Hold the folds together so that you cut through them all, but remember to leave some of the fold intact at the top and the bottom.
- Do the same at the other folded edge.
- Open your strip carefully to see the pattern you have cut in the strip.
- You should find that because the strip was folded, the shapes you cut repeat themselves in the pattern.
- Choose two more coloured strips and cut them in the same way.
- Arrange all three strips on a black piece of card, edge to edge underneath each other. Leave a space between each strip.
- Stick your strips down carefully.

Developing the Idea

- Use the same colour of strip each time but make different cuts on each one.
- Use four strips, two of each colour, repeat the same cut on the matching coloured strips .Stick the strips down alternating the colours.
- Fold a strip more than twice before cutting a pattern.
- Re fold a strip after cutting a pattern and add more cuts to make the repeat pattern more intricate.
- Cut shapes on your strip that are taken from the designs of another culture.
- Cut repeating shapes taken from the environment e.g roof tops. Add drawing to develop the shapes after the row has been stuck down.

Links with AT2 (Knowledge & Understanding of Other Artists)

Border patterns on textiles.
Border patterns on the pages of books.
Border patterns on wallpaper.

Collage

Session Four.

Activity Folding, cutting and decorating circle patterns.

Focus Shape, pattern.

Equipment Needed Doilies, circle shapes to draw round, scissors, glue, glue spreaders, A4 and A3 Black paper, Newsprint or Free Art 80 gsm. Coloured felt tip pens, pencils,coloured sticky paper and coloured sticky paper pre-cut shapes, feathers, coloured foil, plus other extras to use for decoration.

Talk About

- The shape of a doily.
- The shapes on a doily that repeat in several places.
- The holes that make a pattern on a doily.
- The shape of the edge of a doily.
- Drawing round a circular shape.
- Cutting the circle out by cutting carefully along the line with a pair of scissors.
- Folding, cutting and decorating the paper circle.
- Where to put the glue and how much to use.

Doing

- Choose a doily, a piece of black A4 paper, some glue and a glue spreader.
- Put some glue carefully on some of the shapes on the back of your doily (watch out for the holes) and stick it in the middle of your black paper.
- Look carefully at one of the shapes on your doily. Colour just that shape carefully using a felt tip pen.
- Use the same felt tip pen to colour the other shapes on your doily that match the one you have coloured in.
- Choose another shape on your doily to decorate. This time use paper, foil or something different for the decoration.
- Decorate any other matching shapes the same way.
- Find two more sorts of repeating shapes and choose how to decorate each sort. Remember it is a repeating pattern each time.
- Now you are going to make your own doily shape to decorate.
- On a piece of white paper, draw carefully round a circular shape and cut it out.
- Fold your circle in half, and then in half again.
- Cut a pattern along the outside edge first, then cut a pattern down each of the folds remembering to leave some of the folds joined together.
- Open your circle and stick it carefully on a piece of black paper. You are now going to decorate it by adding more repeating patterns. Start with the ones you have already made by cutting, e.g drawing round them, sticking the same shape on them etc.
- Finally, add some more repeating patterns of your own using foil, feathers etc.

Developing the Idea

- Decorate your doily or cut circle using the same colour family for all your repeating patterns.
- Decorate using circle shapes only, -large and small, next to each other, around each other and on top of each other,some with holes in and some without.
- Decorate in the same way but use square shapes instead.

Links with AT2 (Knowledge & Understanding of Other Artists)

Polish paper cuts.
Designs on ceramic and paper plates.

Collage

Session Five.

Activity Paper Skills - curling, fanning, twisting etc.

Focus Shape, pattern and texture.

Equipment Needed Scissors, glue, glue spreaders, long and short strips(between 10 and 20 cm) of fairly stiff paper in various colours about 2cm wide, a square piece of white card to use as the background (20x20cm) or a paper plate.

Talk About

- Changing the shape of the paper strips without cutting them.
- How to fold and re-fold paper to create a zig - zag.
- How to curl paper using scissors or a pencil.
- How to twist and create wavy strips as the paper is stuck down.
- Where to put the glue and how much to use.
- Other ideas for changing paper strips.

Doing

- Choose a long paper strip and zig - zag it by folding it.
- Now choose a short paper strip and zig - zag that too.
- Make some more long and short zig - zags.
- Choose a long paper strip and curl it using scissors or wrapping it round a pencil.
- Do the same with a short paper strip.
- Make some more long and short paper curls.
- Take another strip, and either a paper plate or a square of card, and some glue and a glue spreader.
- You are going to turn this into a wavy strip as you stick it down.
- Glue down one edge on to your paper plate or card square, make a loop before gluing down the next bit of the strip, now make another loop and repeat. Use up all of the strip this way.
- Now you are going to add a twisted strip. Take another strip of paper, glue one end on to your piece of card or paper plate, twist the strip before you glue down the other end. You could add more than one twist if you wanted.
- Finally add your long and short curls and zig - zags to the design.Think carefully about how you are going to arrange them, and where you must put the glue.

Developing the Idea

- Make a collage of curls only.
- Make a collage of zig - zags only.
- Make a wavy line collage.
- Make a collage using only twists.
- Try these paper skills using other sorts of paper e.g. foil
- Make a colour family collage using different papers and different paper skills.
- Make a paper skills collage to decorate a box.

Links with AT2 (Knowledge & Understanding of Other Artists)

Decorated masks from other cultures.
Decorated gift boxes.

Collage

Session SIx.

Activity Finding and matching shapes and colours.

Focus Colour and shape.

Equipment Needed Scissors, glue, glue spreaders, coloured papers, A3 or A4 Newsprint or Free Art 80 gsm. A copy of the Matisse collage 'The Snail.'

Talk About

- The picture and what it reminds them of - before you tell them the actual title.
- Who the artist was.
- The media used by the artist.
- The shapes and colours used by the artist.
- Working in a similar way to the artist and using the same materials.
- Cutting, arranging and sticking.
- Where to put the glue and how much to use.
- Other pictures by the same artist.

Doing

- Find papers that match the colours in the picture by Matisse.
- Cut them into similar shapes. Count them and match them carefully.
- Choose a piece of white paper as your background and arrange your shapes on it. Although you are using the same colours as Matisse you must arrange them in a different way.
- Stick your shapes down when you are happy with the arrangement.
- Give your collage a title .
- Copy the collage picture of 'The Snail' but use different colours from Matisse. Give it a new title.
- Make a collage of your own in a spiral shape.

Developing the Idea

- Choose another Matisse collage, select some of the colours and shapes to use in a collage of your own or select shapes to use but choose your own colours.
- Cut out some of the shapes you can see on a plant - individual shapes, not the whole plant.
- Use the shapes to make a design of your own. Stick them down on a background paper.
- Make a class or group collage based on plant shapes.
- Use the same approach to collage but based on the shapes and patterns seen on the sole of a shoe.

Links with AT2 (Knowledge & Understanding of Other Artists)

Matisse collage pictures.
Wallpaper design.
Wrapping paper design.

Materials

Scissors
Glue
Glue Spreaders

Grey sugar paper
Black sugar paper and card
Free art paper 80 gsm or Newsprint
Sugar paper (assorted colours)
Tissue paper
Coloured sticky paper
Foil
Sequins
Feathers
Ribbons
Doilies
Felt
Textile pieces
Yarns
Margarine tub
Aerosol lids
Paper plates

Suppliers

NES Arnold Ltd
Ludlow Hill Road
West Bridgeford
NOTTINGHAM
NG2 6HD

Pisces
Westwood Studies
West Avenue
CREWE
Cheshire
CW1 3AD

Philip & Tracey Ltd
North Way
Andover
Hampshire
SP10 5BA

Hope Education
Orb Mill
Huddersfield Road
OLDHAM
Lancashire
OL4 2ST

Yorkshire Purchasing Organisation
41 Industrial Park
WAKEFIELD
WF2 0XE

Sculpture

Sculpture

Session One.

Activity Undoing and re -arranging junk materials.

Focus Shape and form.

Equipment Needed Scissors, glue, glue spreaders, cardboard boxes that range in size from Cornflake box size to Oxo cube box size, cardboard rolls, squares of card to attach the construction to(25x25cm), brown gummed parcel tape.

Talk About

- Choosing one box or cardboard roll only to start with. Where and how to change its shape by cutting bits out and re-attaching them somewhere else on the roll or box.
- What sort of shapes to cut out.
- How to re-attach them e.g. glue, tape, or slots.
- How to hold scissors and to cut safely into a box or a cardboard roll.

Doing

- Choose a cardboard box, or a cardboard roll, and a pair of scissors.
- Look at it carefully and decide where you are going to cut some pieces out.
- Decide what shapes they are going to be e.g. strips, circles, pointed shapes etc. Remember they can be both large shapes and small shapes.
- Remember, as you cut bits out your box or cardboard roll, they will be changing shape.
- When you have cut out several shapes, put them together in a pile. You will need them later.
- Glue what is left of your cardboard box or cardboard roll on to a square of card.
- Look carefully at the shapes you have cut out, you are going to re-attach them to a new part of your stuck down box or roll.
- You will need to decide where they are going to go, and how and what you are going to use to re-attach them - glue, tape or slots or all of them.
- You will have made a re-arranged cardboard sculpture.

Developing the Idea

- Make a combined group or class sculpture by attaching and linking work stuck down on a large sheet of card.
- Make individual or group sculptures in which each child uses the same type of junk e.g. egg boxes or cardboard rolls.
- Use paper skills and paint to add decoration.

Links with AT2 (Knowledge & Understanding of Other Artists)

Totem pole designs.
Masks from other parts of the world.
Head dresses for celebrations in other parts of the world.

Sculpture

Session Two.

Activity Adding and inventing using junk material.

Focus Shape, form, colour and texture.

Equipment Needed Boxes (shoe box size) to work inside, scissors, glue, glue spreaders, assorted small junk to fit inside the shoe box, materials for decoration e.g. doilies, tissue paper, ribbon, feathers etc.Ready mix paint, card board pieces to use as palettes, thick and thin brushes.

Talk About

- Choosing a piece of junk to stick inside your shoe box.
- Deciding where it will be stuck and how to stick it down, i.e. where to put the glue and how much to use.
- What this piece of junk could be changed into, e.g. an animal, a vehicle, a person etc by adding to it and decorating it.
- The materials to use for adding and decorating.
- What the background in the box could be.

Doing

- Choose a shoe box and the smaller piece of junk which you are going to fasten inside it.
- Try this piece of junk in several places. When you are happy with where it is going to go glue it down inside your box.
- Look at the shape of your junk carefully and the collage and other junk materials you have to choose from and decide how you are going to change your stuck down junk into something new. What is it going to become, and how you are going to do it?
- When you are ready, choose the other materials you are going to add on. They may need cutting or folding before you use them.
- Stick the extra bits on, you might want to paint some parts as well, then think about adding a background for your creation, e.g.an under water scene if the junk has been added to and become a fish.
- A paper bag - with a rolled up piece of card inside it to make it stand upright -could be added to and decorated in a similar way, e.g. it could become a witch, a clown a self- portrait etc.

Developing the Idea

- All junk creations to link to the same theme e.g. monsters.
- All children to have the same colours, shapes, sizes and amounts of identical junk and additional material.
- Change the junk to match something found in an artists painting, e.g. the colours shapes etc. to match those used by the artist.
- The paper bags could be decorated and linked to a theme e.g. aliens.
- Also they could become 3D portraits in the style of an artist, e.g. Picasso.

Links with AT2 (Knowledge & Understanding of Other Artists)

Picasso.
Totem pole designs.
Photographs of fish, butterflies, insects etc.

Sculpture

Session

Three.

Activity

Wrapping, padding and covering junk material using Modroc.

Focus

Shape and form.

Equipment Needed

Newspaper, brown gummed tape or masking tape, boxes plastic bottles and cardboard rolls. Modroc cut into strips approximately 25cm long, a plastic bowl or ice cream container for water, plastic covering for the Modroc table and where the models are to dry.

Talk About

- How to scrunch newspaper and how to make large and small newspaper parcels.
- Fastening the newspaper parcels with tape.
- Taping the parcels on to the junk.
- What Modroc is and how to use it.
- Only working with it at the the Modroc table and only using it after the junk model has been made and wrapped.
- Cleaning up afterwards.

Doing

- Choose a piece of junk material and some newspaper.
- Make some newspaper parcels and some scrunched newspaper balls.
- Fasten some of them on to your junk in different places using tape.
- Make sure they are fastened on firmly.
- Now carry your model to the Modroc table.
- Pick up a piece of dry Modroc, dip it in the water for just a little while until it becomes soft.
- Lift the Modroc out of the water and wrap it over both the newspaper parcels and the junk material.
- You will need to use several pieces the same way until your model is completely covered. Smooth the Modroc down as you work. Some of the pieces may overlap slightly.
- Leave it to dry on the covered drying surface. It won't take long to dry. When it is ready, paint it in your favourite colours.

Developing the Idea

- The sculptures could become magic stones that need to be painted in magic colours. The children would need to discuss what magic colours are and how to make them to paint their stones.
- The stone shapes could be painted in the colours that match those seen on actual pebbles. The real pebbles could be included in the final display.
- The junk and Modroc constructions could be made to match the shape of coral or barnacles.
- The initial junk and modroc constructions could be further added to and decorated with a range of material (foil, art straws, pipe cleaners etc.) to become, e.g. imaginary creatures.

Links with AT2 (Knowledge & Understanding of Other Artists)

Antoni Gaudi (architecture).
Fredreich Hundertwasser (architecture).

Sculpture

Session Four.

Activity Exploring wire by bending, twisting and looping it.

Focus Line and shape.

Equipment Needed Flexiwire or pipe cleaners, squares of card (15x15 cm), plasticene.

Talk About

- Making the wire safe by bending over a piece at each end to avoid sharp points.
- How to hold the wire with one hand and bend it with the other.
- Shapes that the wire can be bent into - like the lines you can draw, e.g. loops, zig-zags e.t.c.
- How to wrap wire round a pencil to make a coil.
- Putting lumps of plasticene on to a card square and pressing them down firmly.
- Pressing the ends of the wire into the plasticene to make the wire sculpture stand up.

Doing

- Choose a piece of wire and fold each end over carefully.
- Now your wire is ready to work with.
- Make a loop somewhere in your wire.
- Choose a second piece of wire, make it safe, then make two loops in this piece. They don't have to be the same size.
- Make some zig -zags in your next piece. Then try wrapping another piece around a pencil several times, when you take it off you should have a coil.
- Choose a piece of card and some plasticene, make some small plasticene balls and press two of them down firmly on your card.
- Leave quite a large space between them.
- Choose one of the pieces of wire you have been working with and press each end into a plasticene ball. This should help it to stand up.
- Do the same to the other three strips of wire you have been working with. As you fasten the other pieces to your card you may want to make them go under and over each other as well as next to each other.
- You have now made a wire sculpture.

Developing the Idea

- Make a sculpture made up of only twists loops and coils of wire.
- Make a spiky, zig -zag sculpture.
- Make a group wire sculpture.
- Make a sculpture in which each wire changes in two different ways.

Links with AT2 (Knowledge & Understanding of Other Artists)

Alberto Giacometti.
Barbara Hepworth.
Alexander Calder (mobiles).

Sculpture

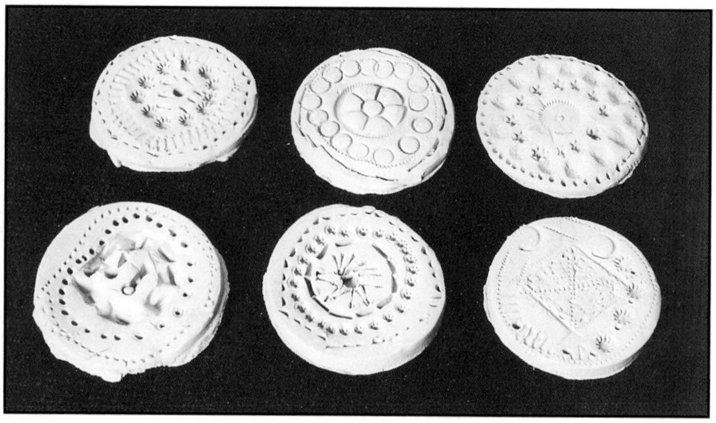

Session Five.

Activity Rolling, cutting and decorating clay tiles.

Focus Shape, texture and pattern.

Equipment Needed Clay rolled into balls about the size of a grapefruit, paper towels to rest on, rolling pins, old wooden rulers to act as rolling guides, assorted junk (keys, screws, shells etc.) to press into the junk to decorate it, plastic knives to cut out the tile shapes. Card squares to use as tile templates.

Talk About

- Putting a ball of clay on a paper towel to stop it sticking to the table.
- Putting a wooden ruler either side of the clay ball.
- How to hold a rolling pin and how to use it to flatten the clay.
- Stopping rolling the clay when the rolling pin is rolling along and touching the wooden rulers.
- Cutting out a tile shape using a plastic knife.
- Decorating the tile by pressing the junk into it to make a pattern.

Doing

- Choose a ball of clay, put it on a paper towel and put a wooden ruler on either side of it.
- Now pick up a rolling pin and begin rolling it over the surface of your clay ball to flatten it.
- You will need to press down firmly.You may need to turn your clay round several times as it flattens and to move the wooden rulers.
- Stop rolling your clay as soon as the rolling pin is touching and rolling on the wooden rulers on both sides of the clay.
- Put away the rulers and the rolling pin.You are now going to cut out a tile shape with a plastic knife.
- Find a card tile template and lay it on you flattened clay, check that there is clay left over all around it.
- Use a plastic knife to draw round your tile template. You will need to press down firmly.
- You should have cut through your rolled out clay, so remove the card template and the extra clay around your cut out shape and discover a tile shaped piece of clay for you to decorate.
- Use a piece of your extra clay to press the junk in and discover the different marks it will make.
- Choose which of these marks you want to use to decorate your tile shape. Arrange the marks to make a pattern e.g. in rows or as a central design with a border pattern around it.
- You can rub the pattern out if it goes wrong or you want to change it by smoothing your finger gently over the surface of the clay.

Developing the Idea

- Cut circular tile shapes to decorate.
- Cut tile shapes based on observation, e.g. leaf shaped tiles or fish shaped tiles.
- Cut face shaped tiles and decorate, re-creating facial features, hair texture etc.
- Each child to cut out and decorate a house shaped tile to become a street scene.

Links with AT2 (Knowledge & Understanding of Other Artists)

Coins.
Actual tiles and books of tile samples.
Wrapping paper with tile like designs.

Sculpture

Session

Six.

Activity

Pulling, pushing and decorating clay shapes.

Focus

Shape and form.

Equipment Needed

Balls of clay about the size of a tennis ball, paper towels to work on, dampened sponges to wet fingers on before smoothing over any cracks, assorted junk (keys, screws, shells etc.) to press into and decorate the clay shapes.

Talk About

- Pulling and pushing shapes out of the same piece of clay.
- Making sure the shapes that are pulled remain part of the starting piece of clay and have not been joined on afterwards.
- What would happen as the clay dries if they had been joined on?
- Pushing and burrowing into the clay carefully to avoid breaking it up.
- Smoothing over any cracks with a finger, first dampening it on the wet sponge.
- Pressing junk onto the clay shape to add pattern and texture.

Doing

- Choose a ball of clay and put it on a paper towel in front of you.
- Change the shape of your clay ball by pulling some shapes out of it. Some could be long and thin whilst others could be short and fat.
- Leave spaces between your pulled shapes and remember they must all be joined to the clay ball you started with. No adding on!
- Now look for spaces on your shape where you can push in and burrow with your finger to make tunnels and holes.
- Smooth over any cracks with a dampened finger.
- Use a small spare bit of clay to find out the marks the junk will make when it is pushed in the clay.
- You are going to use some of these marks to decorate parts of your shape. You will need to be careful where and how firmly you press or your shape will collapse.
- When you know what marks you want to use look carefully at your shape, decide where you are going to put them - and start .

Developing the Idea

- Make a thin decorated shape starting the same way as before, i.e. pulling and burrowing before adding decoration.
- Make a similar but fat decorated shape.
- Make a group collection of thin shapes - each one must be slightly different.
- Make a group of curved decorated shapes -each one must be slightly different.
- Make an animal or a person by pushing and pulling a lump of clay. Add decoration.
- Work from observation and push and pull the shape of a shell or a fir cone from a lump of clay. Add the patterns and textures you see.

Links with AT2 (Knowledge & Understanding of Other Artists)

Henry Moore.
Antoni Gaudi (architecture).
China ornaments.

Materials

Newclay or Buff School clay or Grey clay
Rolling pins
Scissors
Card (4 sheet thickness)
Glue
Glue spreaders
Readymix or powder paint
Palettes/Inking trays
Foil
Doilies
Sticky paper
Brown paper gummed tape
Modroc
Flexi wire
Plasticene
Paper bags (Rainbow bags from NES Arnold)
Shoe boxes or box lid A4 size
Newspaper
Wooden rulers
Assorted Junk (Keys, screws, etc.)

Suppliers

NES Arnold Ltd
Ludlow Hill Road
West Bridgeford
NOTTINGHAM
NG2 6HD

Pisces
Westwood Studies
West Avenue
CREWE
Cheshire
CW1 3AD

Philip & Tracey Ltd
North Way
Andover
Hampshire
SP10 5BA

Hope Education
Orb Mill
Huddersfield Road
OLDHAM
Lancashire
OL4 2ST

Yorkshire Purchasing Organisation
41 Industrial Park
WAKEFIELD
WF2 0XE

Sculpture

Session 1
Example of re-arranging junk materials into totem pole designs.

Session 2
Example of adding and inventing inside a box.

Session 3
Example of wrapping, padding, and covering junk using Modroc.

Sculpture

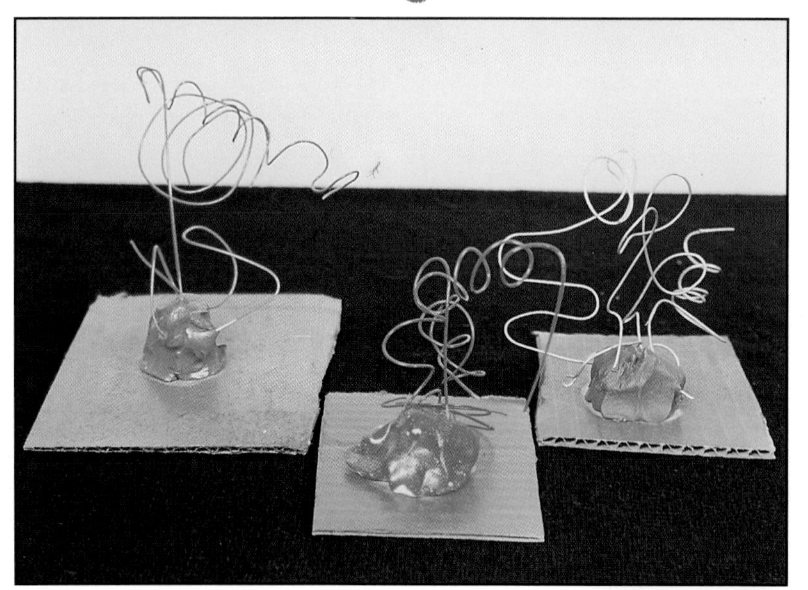

Session 4
Example of exploring wire by bending, twisting and looping.

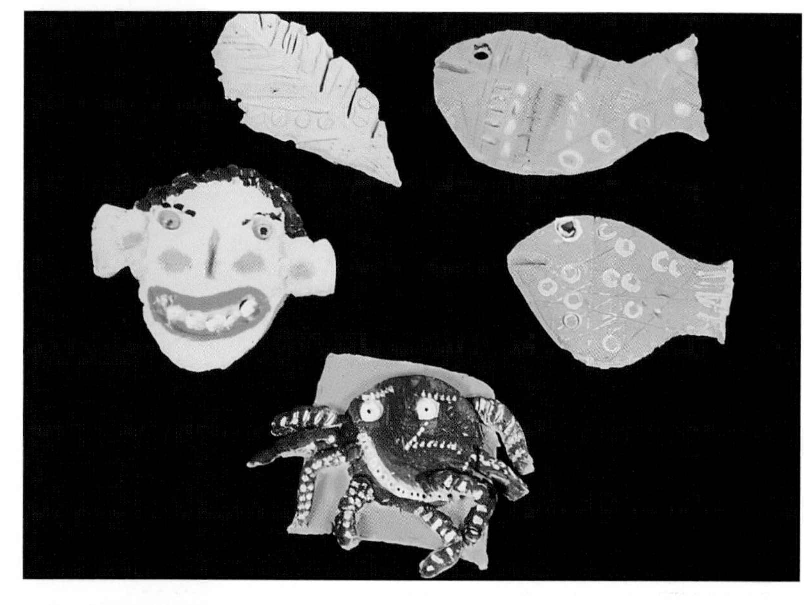

Session 5
Example of rolling, cutting and decorating clay tiles.

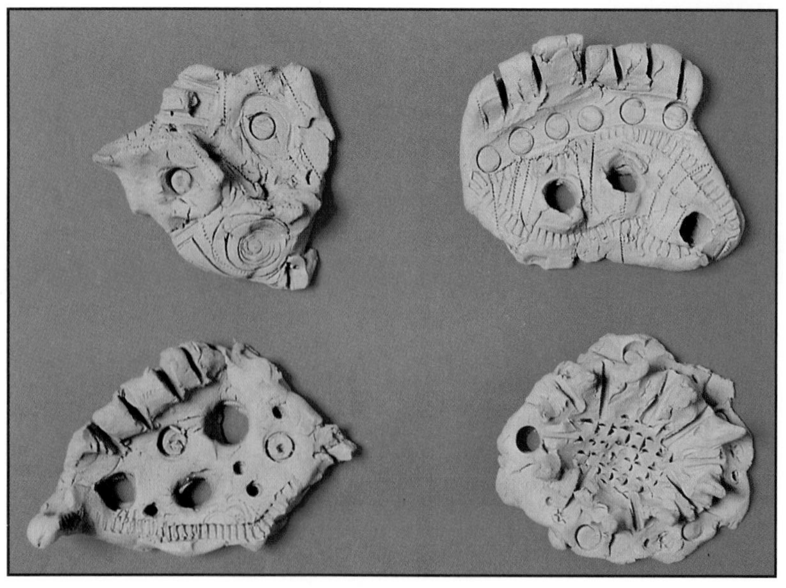

Session 6
Example of pulling, pushing and decorating clay shapes.

Textiles

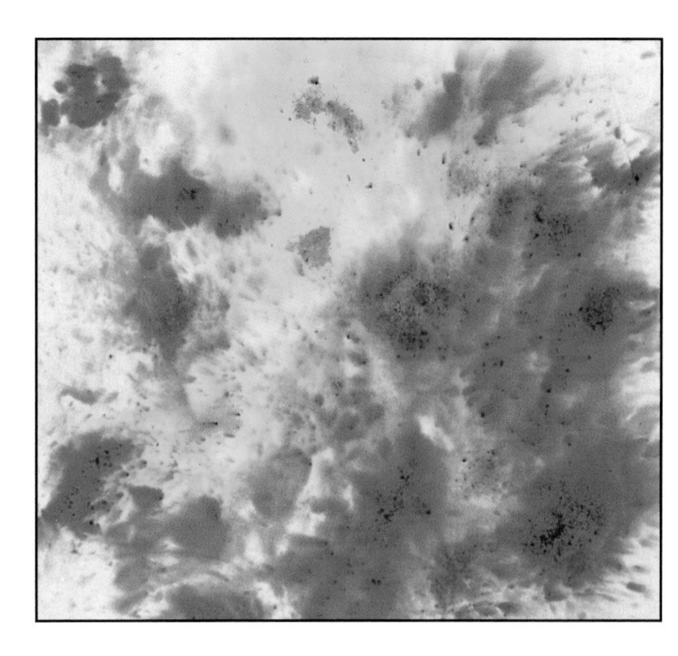

Session 1
Example of colouring textiles using powdered dye.

Session 2
Example of drawing, painting and masking out.

Session 3
Examples of draw a line, stitch a line.

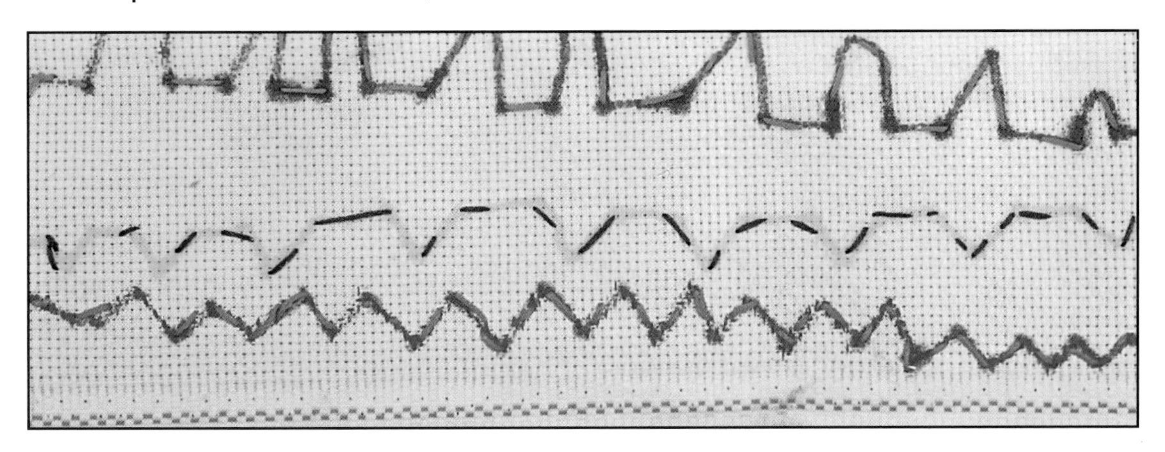

Textiles

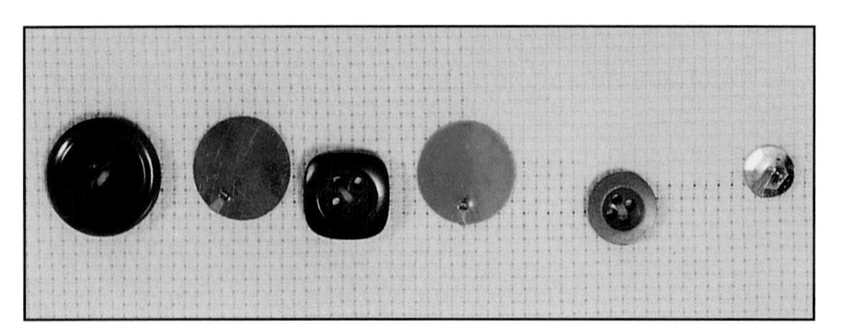

Session 4
Example of adding on buttons, beads and sequins.

Session 5
Example of changing a design by drawing and sticking.

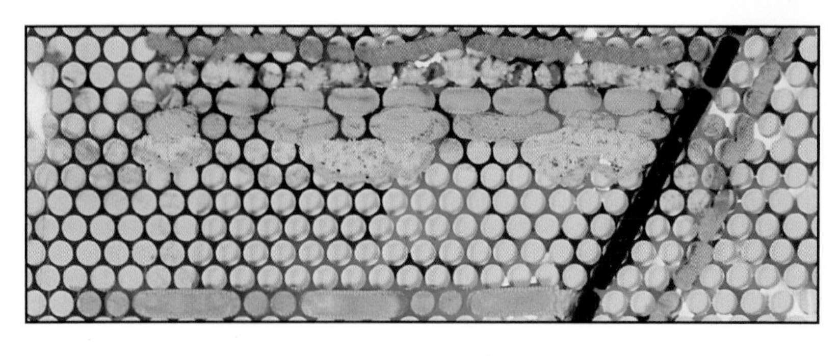

Session 6
Example of simple weaving using sequin waste.

Textiles

Textiles

Session One.

Activity Colouring textiles using dye.

Focus Colour and pattern.

Equipment Needed Tubs of Brusho or Easibrush dyes with pepper pot type holes punched in the lids, plain white cotton fabric cut into squares approximately 12x12 cm, a bowl of water, a windolene type spray bottle or plant mister filled with water, protective covering on the table.

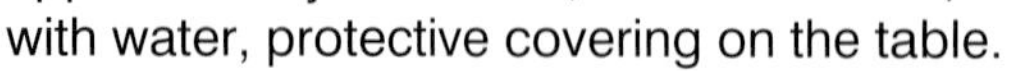

Talk About

- How to wet the fabric.
- Laying the fabric out flat.
- Shaking the tub of powdered dye downwards onto the fabric.
- Using lots of different colours on the same fabric.
- Taking care as dye will stain.

Doing

- Choose a piece of fabric, and dip it in the bowl of water.
- Squeeze out the fabric and lay it flat on a folded up newspaper on your table.
- Choose a tub of dye.
- Shake and sprinkle the dye downwards on to the fabric.
- In a while the colour should begin to spread.
- Sprinkle other colours, one at a time until the fabric has become a multi-coloured textile.
- Choose a second piece of fabric, wet it and lay it out as before on some more folded newspaper.
- Sprinkle one one colour of dye, now spray some extra water on to the fabric using the windolene spray bottle or plant mister. This will help to spread the dye.
- Sprinkle some more colours on the same fabric and spray them with water too. Some of the colours should have merged together.

Developing the Idea

- Sprinkle your fabric with warm colours of dye only.
- Sprinkle your fabric with cold colours of dye only.
- Sprinkle your fabric in the colours seen in an artist's picture.
- Sprinkle your fabric in the colours of a season.
- Use the sprinkled fabric as the background for a picture made up of other fabric pieces that have been stuck on, e.g. a garden full of flowers.

Links with AT2 (Knowledge & Understanding of Other Artists)

The Impressionists for the build up of colour rather than the outline of shapes.
Georges Seurat (Pointillism).
The Fauvists (Derain, Dufy etc.), for the use of strong colour like those found in the dyes.

Textiles

Session Two.

Activity Drawing, painting and masking out.

Focus Colour, shape and pattern.

Equipment Needed Plain white cotton fabric cut into squares approximately 12x12 cm, masking tape, pre-cut shapes of sticky backed plastic without the backing removed, dye stick fabric crayons, fabric paint, paint brushes, card pieces to use as palettes and fabric felt tip pens.

Talk About

- Arranging and sticking sticky backed plastic shapes or strips of masking tape on to the fabric to keep parts of it white.
- Colouring over the covered areas as well as the fabric itself using the dye sticks.
- Pressing on firmly to add plenty of colour.
- Drawing lines and patterns as well.
- Removing the sticky backed plastic shapes or masking tape.
- Decorating the white shapes using paint or felt tips or both.

Doing

- Choose a piece of fabric and several pre-cut sticky back plastic shapes or a roll of masking tape.
- Arrange the sticky back shapes in several ways before you decide how you are going to stick them down. Peel off the backing and press them on to your fabric, sticky side downwards!
- If you are using masking tape instead you will need to cut one strip at a time and press each one on to the fabric sticky side down. The strips don't all have to meet, but they can cross over if you want them to. Remember to leave plenty of space to colour on.
- Now choose the dye stick colours to use and add plenty of colour to your fabric by pressing on firmly all the time. Remember to go over the covered up bits as well.
- Take off the tape or sticky backed plastic. You should now have some white shapes to decorate. If you want, you could outline the shapes with a fabric felt pen or a dye stick first.
- Think carefully about how you are going to decorate your white shapes using paint, and fabric felt pen. Some of the shapes could be filled in whilst others could have patterns on them.

Developing the Idea

- Colour in each shape with the same colour.
- Colour the fabric in cold colours and the shapes in warm colours.
- Colour the fabric in warm colours and the shapes in cold colours.
- Use cut shapes or masking tape to make a fish or flower design on the fabric - colour over the top, remove the plastic or tape then decorate the flower or fish itself.
- Stick a series of leaf shapes on to the fabric,colour it in autumn colours then decorate the white leaf shapes with patterns in autumn colours.
- Cut a hand shape out of sticky backed plastic and stick it on to the fabric. Colour over the top. Decorate the white hand shape with Menhdi style patterns.

Links with AT2 (Knowledge & Understanding of Other Artists)

Stencil designs.
Menhdi patterns.

Textiles

Session Three.

Activity Draw a line, stitch a line.

Focus Line, pattern and texture.

Equipment Needed Needles with fairly large eyes for easy threading, coloured hessian or similar open weave fabric about A4 size, assorted coloured threads cut into various lengths, each one having a knot at the end, dye sticks for drawing on the fabric.

Talk About

- Different sorts of lines
- Drawing lines on fabric.
- Holding, threading and using a needle to make a stitch.
- Following a drawn line with a stitched line.
- Sewing through a loop to finish off.
- Putting the needle away safely.

Doing

- Choose a piece of fabric and a dye stick to draw with.
- Draw a line with a zig-zag in it somewhere on your fabric.
- Pick up a needle and some coloured thread.
- Thread your needle, put it underneath your fabric and push it up through your fabric at the beginning of your drawn line.
- You are now going to sew stitches along this line until you get to the end.
- Make a loop with your thread and push your needle through it to finish off. Pull the loop together and cut off your thread.
- Draw another zig-zag line and stitch on top of it with a different colour.
- Draw a third zig zag line, but sew under it this time and not on it using a different colour thread.
- Your stitched line should match the coloured line you have drawn.

Developing the Idea

- Draw a different sort of line each time on your fabric, stitch on some and under others using lots of different colours.
- Draw several similar lines on your fabric and stitch on and under them in different colours, use long stitches only or short stitches only for each line.
- Draw several similar lines on your fabric, some close together and some far apart. Add some stitched lines on and under these lines where you would like. Leave some gaps as well.
- Collect lines from an artists drawing to draw and copy in stitches.
- Collect lines from a leaf or piece of bark to draw and copy in stitches.
- Draw water pattern lines to copy in stitches.

Links with AT2 (Knowledge & Understanding of Other Artists)

Vincent van Gogh.
Jan Beaney.
Samplers.
Embroidery design books.

Textiles

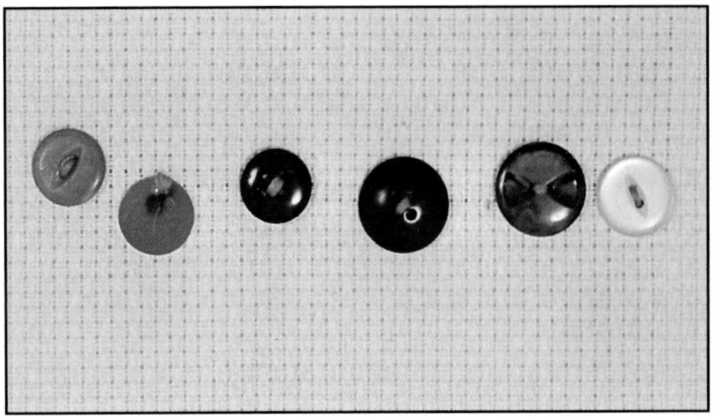

Session Four.

Activity Adding on buttons, beads and sequins.

Focus Pattern shape and colour.

Equipment Needed Strips of hessian or similar loose weave fabric about 22cm long and 8 cm wide, needles with large eyes for easy threading, assorted coloured threads cut to varying lengths with a knot at the end, dye sticks for drawing dots, an assortment of buttons, sequins and beads, small paper plates.

Talk About

- Choosing and arranging sequins, beads or buttons on your fabric strip.
- Marking where they are to go with a drawn dot.
- How to hold, thread and use a needle.
- Pushing the needle up through the fabric, then through the hole in the button, bead or sequin and back in the fabric again and pulling it tight.
- Pushing the needle up through the next mark to add on the next button, bead or sequin.
- Finishing off at the end of the row by making a loop and pulling the needle through it before cutting off the thread.

Doing

- Choose a coloured strip of fabric and a collection of about six buttons, or beads or sequins. It can be an mixture of all three, or a combination of just two sorts, e.g. 3 buttons and 3 beads.
- Arrange them on your fabric in a row with spaces between each one. You may want to try several arrangements until you are satisfied.
- Now use a dye stick to make a dot where each one is going to be sewn.
- Move the buttons, beads and sequins into a pile away from the fabric. It would be a good idea to put them on a paper plate so that they don't get lost.
- Pick up a needle and thread it with coloured cotton, then put it under the fabric and push it up through the first dot you have drawn.
- Choose a button, bead or sequin and thread the needle through the hole in it and then push the needle back into the fabric close to the dot you had come through before.
- If you have chosen a button it will probably have more than one hole in it. Push the needle up through one of the holes and down through a second one as you fasten it on to the fabric.
- To add your second button, bead or sequin, push your needle up through the second dot you have drawn and fasten it on as before.
- Continue the same way until you have fastened on all your button, beads and sequins.
- Finish off by sewing through a loop, pull it tight and then cut off the thread.

Developing the Idea

- Add sequins, buttons or beads that are all the same colour.
- Stick some circles of coloured fabric down on a strip, leaving a gap between each one. Sew a bead or button on each circle and a sequin in each gap.
- Stick and sew a different pattern of your own.
- Work on a patterned piece of fabric and use the repeats in the pattern to help you arrange your decoration.

Links with AT2 (Knowledge & Understanding of Other Artists)

Patterns on the costumes of Pearly Kings and Queens.
Woven bags or hand bags decorated with buttons.

Textiles

Session Five.

Activity Changing a design by drawing, sewing and sticking.

Focus Colour, shape and pattern.

Equipment Needed Beads, buttons and sequins, squares of patterned fabric 18x18 cm approximately. Dye sticks, pre-cut small circles, squares and triangles of coloured felt, needles with large eyes for easy threading, assorted coloured threads of varying lengths each with a knot at the end. Fabric glue sticks - these are less messy than other glues.

Talk About

- The patterns on the pieces of fabric.
- The shapes and colours in the patterns.
- Where the patterns could be added to.
- What could be added to them.
- How they could be added - by sticking, sewing and drawing.

Doing

- Choose a piece of fabric and look carefully at the pattern on it.
- Find one shape that is repeated in the pattern and add the same sort of felt shape to each one. Fasten them down with glue.
- Look for another group of repeating shapes. You might want to decorate these by drawing.
- See if you can find some shapes that you could decorate by stitching or sewing on beads etc.
- You might like to sew beads etc. on to some of the felt shapes you have stuck on or to stick smaller felt shapes on top of the larger ones.
- There are lots of ways you can change the pattern you started with, but remember to think about the repeats. Remember, your changed pattern must still be a repeating pattern.

Developing the Idea

- Create a repeat patterned fabric of your own, starting with a plain piece of fabric and adding repeated felt shapes, drawing and stitching.
- Stick patterned and plain fabric shapes as a repeating pattern on a plain background and add further decoration.
- Use one way of decorating for the plain fabric and a different way for the patterned pieces.
- Stick a circle of plain fabric in the centre of a plain background and add patterned pieces round it. Decorate the plain fabric with beads etc. Think of a way you can decorate on and around the patterned fabric.

Links with AT2 (Knowledge & Understanding of Other Artists)

Patchwork quilt designs.
Banner designs.